1 2 95

A BIBLE OF YOUR OWN

A BIBLE OF YOUR OWN

Growing with the Scriptures

by Han Renckens, S.J.

Translated by
Nancy Forest-Flier

ORBIS BOOKS
Maryknoll, New York 10545

The Catholic Foreign Mission Society of America (Maryknoll) recruits and trains people for overseas missionary service. Through Orbis Books, Maryknoll aims to foster the international dialogue that is essential to mission. The books published, however, reflect the opinions of their authors and are not meant to represent the official position of the society.

English translation by Nancy Forest-Flier, edited by Toni Sortor and William R. Burrows, copyright © 1995 Orbis Books, Maryknoll, New York 10545.

Published in the United States by Orbis Books, Maryknoll, New York. Original Dutch edition, *Je eigen Schrift schrijven: Meegroeien met de bijbel* ("Write Your Own Scripture: Growing with the Bible"), published in 1983 by Uitgeverij Ambo bv Baarn, Netherlands. Published in Great Britain by Gracewing, Fowler-Wright Books Ltd., Herefordshire, England.

Manufactured in the United States of America.

Library of Congress Cataloging-in-Publication Data

Renckens, Han.
    [Je eigen Schrift schrijven. English]
    A Bible of your own : growing with the Scriptures / by Han Renckens : translated by Nancy Forest-Flier : [edited by Toni Sortor and William R. Burrows].
       p. cm.
    ISBN 1-57075-007-6 (paper) : $10.95
    1. Bible—Introductions. 2. Bible—Devotional use. 3. Judaism (Christian theology) I. Sortor, Toni, 1939- . II. Burrows, William R. III. Title.
BS475.2.R46   1995
220.6'1—dc20   94-45525
                                          CIP

ORBIS/ISBN 1-57075-007-6
GRACEWING/ISBN 0-85244-319-6

Contents

Part 3
THE STUDY HOUSE OF THE WORD

Editor's Foreword

I first learned of Han Renckens, S.J., and the remark-able, challenging, book you have in your hand, *A Bible of Your Own,* in June 1991, while attending the meeting of the board of the journal *Concilium* near Budapest. I was walking in the hills overlooking the Danube with John Coleman, S.J., talking about good books. Accord-ing to John, "Renckens makes everything you've read in and about the Bible come together . . . one of the best books on Scripture I've ever read." Later that week, I asked Father Bas van Iersel, a New Testament exegete of immense learning and renown, what he thought of the book. "If there is any book I could be jealous of another man writing, it is that one," said Bas. "It is absolutely amazing how much Renckens has been able to put between those covers."

At the Frankfurt Book Fair several months later, the Dutch publisher said the same thing, adding that *A Bible of Your Own* had also been an extraordinary sales success. I then asked for reviews of the book from my friends and Orbis authors Joseph Donders, M.Afr., and Robert

Schreiter, C.Pp.S., the former Dutch by birth, the latter
an American who had studied in Holland. Seldom have
I received reader reports so glowing.

And thus began the process that led to Orbis translat-
ing *Je eigen Schrift schrijven: Meegroeien met de bijbel*
(literally, "A Scripture of Your Own: Growing with the
Bible"). Permission processes took time, and so did the
translation. When I could at last read the book, I found
myself impressed and taught by Han Renckens in ways
I had hardly expected. Renckens has managed to distill
scholarly insights from decades of exegetical work into
a book without footnotes. Taken together, at one level
Renckens shows that the Bible authorizes, indeed *requires*, that each age take seriously its own history as
sacred. At another level, he puts flesh on the bones of
the saying, "Jews are our elder brothers and sisters in
faith."

A Bible of Your Own is a daring book. It believes that
the New Testament is a postscript to the "Old Scriptures" and shows that virtually every Christian theological truism bearing on Jewish-Christian relations is
misleading at best, dangerous at worst. Ultimately,
Renckens raises the following important questions:

- Should Christians regard Judaism and the Covenant with the Jews as theologically valid *today?*
- If so, what about Christian mission to Jews *today?*

Ancient Judaism is treated with great nuance and
sympathy by Christian scholars, a Jewish friend—him-

self the author of numerous books—observed, but they have a hard time saying clearly that they view *contemporary post-biblical Judaism as theologically integral.* Jews for their part have a hard time dealing theologically with who Jesus is, my friend notes, and they need to do this. *A Bible of Your Own* is a powerful reminder that Jewish-Christian understanding and dialogue need to move to an entirely new level if it is to escape the accusation that its partners are trapped in an ecumenical embrace that keeps them from asking the hard questions.

Though written without footnotes, *A Bible of Your Own* is a demanding work, and the scholarship that stands behind it is impeccable ... I do not know if Father Renckens knows Alfred North Whitehead's axiom that the most important insights can be shown to be compelling but not proved true. But what Han Renckens *shows* is that the most important result of the deepest and best biblical scholarship frees us from the tyranny of scholars to appropriate the message that "our earthly existence is for each of us a personal mission and a promise of God's providence. Human beings become believers when they discover and meet this God of their own history, when they honor and love God by being faithful to the particular promise and mission that are made possible in their own circumstances."

The implications of this book in a host of areas are immense—ethics, mission, interreligious relations, spirituality, inculturation, and so forth. In the last issue, for instance, how can one justify insisting upon theological language shaped by Western developments? Why follow determinations from far away on the shape Christian communities should take in local, non-Western contexts? Father Renckens' view of the scriptural process authorizes a variety of approaches to such questions without predetermining the outcome.

A Bible of Your Own was a difficult book to translate and edit. The Dutch style is richly allusive. It abounds in folksy metaphors and expressions, and that makes capturing its meaning an elusive task. Nancy Forest-Flier did yeoman work, however, in capturing it. Father Renckens read her translation and offered suggestions. He has also read and approved the edition of his work you are about to read, in which the attempt has been to make explicit for an English-speaking audience what was implicit in the richness of the original. Kathleen M. O'Connor read the edited translation and made many helpful corrections, both small and large. Finally, Toni Sortor's painstaking editorial skills are found on every page of this edition.

William R. Burrows

Preface

And they believed the scriptures and the word that Jesus had spoken . . .

(John 2:22)

This little book is about what the Bible itself, particularly in the New Testament, names "the Scriptures," the books sometimes called "Old Testament," the authentic and original Holy Bible called here "the Old Scriptures."

First an observation. "There's belief and then there's *belief*," especially where the Bible is concerned. What, though, is the *proper* way to believe *in the Scriptures?* How did the disciples believe? Belief definitely did not come with the first word they heard. For them, at a certain moment lights went on and everything was different.

In any case, there is a way to approach the Bible that will lead to the formation of opinions, sometimes even great and inspiring opinions. Such conjecture-type opinions begin to dawn on us when we straightforwardly examine how the Old Scriptures developed.

"Straightforward" our journey may be, but it certainly isn't an exercise devoid of emotion. In a deeply moving history lasting a thousand years, the Scriptures grew into a fossilized book, an immovable monument that today is already two thousand years old. Reverence toward biblical pronouncements tends to lead to immovability, grim orthodoxy, and the kind of misunderstandings that commonly occur when the books of the Bible are not seen in their original contexts.

Correcting that grim orthodox family of misunderstandings is what the first thousand years of biblical history are good for! And we don't have to go far to learn about this history, for the Scriptures themselves are the principal source of information. They have a great deal to tell us about their own growth, not in so many words, but chiefly through what they are and what they have proven to be in their entire fascinating form.

Seen the way we hope to show in this book, the Scriptures are not a matter of obligation but of "permission," in the ironic sense, first, that they are permitted to exist at all. Second, that you are permitted to encounter them, to be with them, to discover that they are yours as well, your book. For then you'll find yourself writing your own Scriptures or, if you prefer, your own "Testament," old or new (it doesn't really matter which).

The activity of writing the Scriptures we call the Bible had a beginning once upon a time. By examining how those first writers accomplished their work, we can learn how to copy their art. The Scriptures' own origins, in other words, point the way to a reliable path that will lead us to understanding.

To keep a better eye on the road ahead, it makes sense to save looking up biblical sites until later.

Part 1 | THE NATURE AND ACTIVITY OF THE WORD

1 | Speaking, Believing, Writing

A popular approach to presenting scriptural material runs together the narrative parts of the Bible in one continuous story. Without disputing the right to follow such an approach, such summaries simply don't do justice to dimensions evoked in one's individual spiritual life or by the real shape of the Bible itself. For this reason we cannot begin without some introductory reflections.

The biblical soil has become tightly compressed under the weight of two thousand years, and a bit of tilling and turning is required to aerate it. Those who suspect that something will be undermined in the process are perfectly correct. But the question is, what are we undermining? The following proposition approaches the question without beating around the bush. Expressed in three ways, I try to make the challenge to biblical studies recognizable, so that no thinking person can avoid it. The principle involved is this: *the Bible is about much more than biblical history.*

First, we should not conclude from the story of the Bible that God was more concerned with people long ago than with us today. Second, if that sounds negative, just turn it around and say: "I am convinced that God is just as intensely involved in our lives today as the Bible so emphatically tells us God was in the past." Or you can put it a third way: Our biblical ancestors would cease to be the fathers and mothers of our faith if God were not just as silent and hidden in their time as in ours.

When God Speaks

There is a saying that goes, "God is silent in every language," a problem well documented in Psalm 10:1-4 and 11. But diametrically opposed to this is the profession of faith: "Our God comes and does not keep silence" (Ps. 50:3 and 21). The Scripture attempts to open our ears to expect God's future advent, so that we can hear the Voice which, even now, fills the silence that surrounds and sometimes oppresses us. The idols are nothing more than dumb things, despite their noisy presence (Ps. 115:4-7).

It is the age-old test of faith: "O God, do not keep silence; do not hold your peace or be still, O God!" (Ps. 83:1; see Pss. 22:1-2; 28:1; 35:22; 39:12; 109:1; Is. 42:14; 57:11; Hab. 1:13). "Where is your God?" (Pss. 42:3; 79:10; Joel 2:17 and also Ps. 22:1 and Wis. 2:18-20 and Mt. 27:43).

The task of the Scriptures is to hold up to readers an

attitude with which they might proceed with their own lives. This is the purpose of the story about the past. The Scriptures recount epochal events that were and still are pure expectations of faith (Judges 6:13). In this respect there is no difference between then and now, although the outer appearance of the story often seems to imply something else.

This way of telling by preaching not only illustrates the contents of faith by making it a comprehensible fact, but it also radiates an infectious certainty. That is to say that prophets are so sure of their business that they see things through God's eyes, they see things in their ultimate completion, even though they're still talking about the future. For this reason they use the past tense when speaking of future visions—the new is already here, it has taken place (Rev. 21:6a).

Even when a biblical story recalls memories from the past it is more or less prophecy in story form with an "eschatological" slant. A story that is stuck in the past—genuinely, and not for the sake of appearances—isn't worth the trouble of retelling or rehearing. There is not one biblical story that contains this kind of disengagement. Rather the story is program, TORAH.

Some of the stories tell us that God spoke—on Mount Sinai, for example. If we respond, "If only I had been there," the story answers: You underestimate your own ability to experience. Sinai is near you and lies within your grasp (Dt. 5:3).

The "word" of God presupposes divine speech. From ancient times it has been said that the speech of God is an "act." God, in this image expresses himself, "reveals" Godself in actions. God speaks through works that must be called God's "word." And for this reason, God's words are never hollow words (Is. 55:8-11).

The observed and experienced reality that we are and that we live, and that occurs on the human plane, is our entrée to the world of the divine—the primordial location of truth, revelation, and "God's will." To draw from this well is to be on the trail of God. One discovers God and gradually forms an idea of God's nature.

Two Entrances

We who "people the earth" don't begin with a blank page. In addition to the channels cut by our own individual existences, we are confronted with what generations before us have learned about God through their experience. They put ideas into words, thus creating a tradition of language and story. This gives us a more defined path to God. Divine activity and presence have been given voice and put into words.

In the history of religious and biblical experience, when our fathers and mothers perceived accurately the inner depths of human existence, their words become classics and are added to the authority of God's own word in a complex process that yields a canon or list of what is judged authentic and reliable. This word, interpreted in bits and pieces, is then brought into circulation, as it were, in manageable small change. "Holy books," bundles and sacks of coins, make up "the word of God" in every religion.

So God's word can be attained along two roads—in tradition and in primal experience and consciousness. Both are, in principle, accessible to us, and we should travel both of them; they depend on each other and we need the product of their interaction. The word of assent in the life of faith is a fundamental and very personal matter that lies in the area of individual responsibility. No one can assent for me. For this reason, all the words of tradition must be held up against and become filled with the living and fundamental word evoked in the inner world of my human consciousness and "conscience." This non-verbal, formless word is woven into my existence as if braided from countless hairs.

The interaction between life and a tradition of words brings faith to the public realm. There it is given shape and direction in the encounter with words prophesied by tradition. We listen reverently and continue to feel our way with growing suspicion, just long enough and with enough patience until the words of living tradition grip our hearts and we begin expressing truth in our own words "from the ground of our being."

The Scriptures as Word

The Old Scriptures profess that God speaks to people and calls them to account for their humanity, their ability to say yes or no to each other, to be open or to be closed. The Old Scriptures see earthly existence as the establishment of a "covenant" between God and humanity. This covenant is made to reflect the connection by which people pay attention to each other's needs, and it can only be realized through this connection.

The Old Scriptures refer to this human situation by speaking about the "land" as both a gift of the covenant and a task of the covenant, that is, the object of a free choice. You can refuse to enter the land—to take up your own place in the midst of humanity—because you are reluctant to do so, as well as because you distrust it and don't believe in it. But then you lose your trust in God. In biblical tradition, I am then confronted with the question, Has the "Lord" brought me "here" not out of love, but because the Lord hates me and wants to destroy me? (Dt. 1:27; Num. 14:1-4; 16:13-14; 20:4-5). Does human life have any meaning? Is it worth the trouble to be what you are? "Is the Lord among us or not?" (Ex. 17:7).

When the Scripture says that God spoke in the past— and this boils down to God saying good things about Israel (Num. 10:29, 32)—it means (and causes me to realize) that God speaks to me now. That is why the Scripture is the pre-eminent word of God. It places the characteristic function of the word—to clarify matters— in the face of the non-verbal reality because its task is to discover ("reveal" to me) my personal life story as the embodiment and location of the divine word. The Scriptures mean to show me that the situation in which I find myself must indeed be interpreted as the word of God.

Jesus as Word

Connected in a practical and demonstrable way with the verbal character of the Scriptures (Gen. 1 and Jn. 1; Heb. 1:1-2), the New Testament, at the last moment, turned "the Word of God" into a title for Jesus. When Jesus is referred to in this way it is meant as both an extension and a finalization, related to the fact that the title was first used for the Old Scriptures.

First and at the very least, this means that all the old words flow together in Jesus Messiah and are made completely true—are "fulfilled"—in Jesus. The Jesus story reveals what the Old Scriptures are leading to and what they want to bind in our hearts. The Old Scriptures' deepest intent is tersely formulated (a common Semitic style) in the contrasting statements of the Sermon on the Mount.

In a more complicated way of approaching this, by identifying God, Word, and Jesus in his prologue (Jn. 1:1-18), it sometimes seems as though St. John throws open a wide new territory merely for speculation. But that is an optical illusion caused by the controversies surrounding christological doctrine. St. John's aim, however, was to bring all the preceding tradition under the tent of his Jesus figure by summarizing it literally in one "word." In short, for John there is but one word of God. It includes both the written Scriptures as well as the Messiah and finds its meaning in *both* of them.

Incarnate and Written Word

This summing up of common characteristic features from the "written" and the "incarnate" word of God is also the aim of tradition. Tradition realizes that the matter at hand is two forms of one word which inform and supplement each other: the word resounds with its full tone only when justice is done to both forms.

In its capacity as the word of God, Scripture has been an object of intensive consideration for the past century. New factual data, which formerly were virtually inaccessible, necessitated renewed reflection and reformulation of Scripture in this role. Christology should take advantage of these insights. To do so, it will have to set out for the hundredth time on the road where it all began in the story of Israel and of Jesus in a different vein. Without that story, christology is empty and Christian theology as a whole becomes mere reified interpretation of events frozen in a dead past. To mine the new vein of insights, theology must pay special attention to the Old Scriptures. Guidance for this task comes from the ancient saying that, "Torah [the Old Scriptures in their entirety] is pregnant with the Messiah."

Indeed, this Scripture is not only an inseparable context. It is also the womb and cradle of Jesus Messiah and, even more, of the Messianic witness. The Old Scriptures are certainly much more than a mere linguistic backdrop to Jesus, as if the New Testament had borrowed from

Old Scriptures in the same way that it borrowed hellenistic terminology.

A famous Semitic saying has it that it is not Mary who is to be called blessed but whoever keeps the word of God (Lk. 11:27-28), thus making Mary's biological motherhood subordinate to her "fertility of belief." This is a golden thread that runs throughout the Scriptures, so that "the Messianic Mother" (Is. 7:14; Mic. 5:2) is both the form and the exponent of the believing community. The Messiah is to be expected as the fruit of Israel-at-its-best (Mt. 12:46-50 and Rev. 12); the Messiah must be embodied in the people themselves. Then He will come.

The relationship between the ancient Scriptures and the New Testament rests on this flow and kinship in belief, the roots of which are indicated by the fourth evangelist. Whoever believes is—in a "virginal domain"—born of God (Jn. 1:12-13). This connection in belief between two peoples, realized in the realm of life itself, takes on literary expression in the realm of Scripture. The features of the Messianic profile in the Old Scriptures flow together into the Jesus figure of the New Testament.

As a Jewish man, Jesus is the fruit of centuries of faithful living. He is "true man," not a divine "know-it-all" (a faulty conclusion drawn from Lk. 2:46-47). He sat on the benches of the study house and read from the Old Scriptures to learn, not to *pretend* to learn. His ancestry goes back to David and Abraham (Mt. 1:1) and is more than a page from the census registry. His ancestry is a concretization of the literary fact that the Old Scriptures are the cradle of the New Testament and of the image of Jesus which the gospels evoke.

What's Old in the New Testament

Classical theology is based more in a history of events frozen in the past on the pages of the Bible than in the biblical vision of God and humans meeting each other in history. Such classical theology works more with the old facts than with the dynamic ideas expressed in the texts when read dynamically. Finally, such theology pays insufficient attention to the common stream of living history revealed in the two Scriptures.

Systematic theology is aware that the New Testament refers to old words, but is often misled by their antiquity and concreteness to treat the Old Scriptures as if the New revealed meanings and worlds that were not available in the Old. Thus misguided, theology sees words in the Old Scriptures talking about "old facts," with meanings long over and done with. And with that move, the New Testament is treated as if its words reveal completely new meanings.

In that view, the Old Scriptures have nothing more to contribute. They are an abandoned building occupied by squatters. The furniture (the language) can be seized by those who care to take it and make themselves comfortable.

By way of contrast, in the view being presented in this

little book, we can't be reminded enough of (what Paul Ricoeur has called) the "surplus of meaning" of the Old Scriptures. They have much to tell us about God, about being a people, and about the Messiah. They cover so many areas of life that the epilogue added by the New Testament literally hasn't a leg to stand on without them. It's no more than a single head, without body or limbs.

When you think of it, the New Testament-as-epilogue is most impressive in the way it accurately extracts what is contained in the Old. The old words should be examined in that light. In much theological practice, however, the Old Scriptures are regarded as offering no substantial foundation to the New Testament. Thus truncating the old words, Christians are led prematurely to embark on philosophical speculative adventures that some layers of the New Testament seem to invite.

Nevertheless, Johannine and especially Pauline reflections, no matter how fascinating and important they may be, are really surface phenomena—products of their age, determined by convention, spiritual climate, and a sort of popular philosophical *patois*. It is safer to resist making too much fuss over the philosophy. Far better to translate it back to the Old Scriptures upon which it is based, as scholars have known for a generation.

Indeed, it is in the Old Scriptures where the new covenant is discovered (Jer. 31:31; 32:40), just as the new heavens and the new earth (Is. 65:17; 62:22) and, above all, the "circumcision of the heart" (Dt. 10:16; 30:6; Jer. 4:4; Ezek. 36:26). A people wrestling with God in their history arrived at these insights as ways of dealing with the redemption they needed to be God's people. They put them into words, because they had experienced the realities signified in them.

Throughout the Old Scriptures the notion is expressed that faith makes old persons new, that the life of faith is *real* life that brings earthly existence to fulfillment.

If the labels "fear" and "love"—which not long ago were used to contrast the "two" Testaments—are today recognized to be both objectionable and inaccurate as characterizations of the Old Scriptures and their epilogue, perhaps the contrast between "old" and "new" misleads just as much. This contrast is, admittedly, to be found within the Old Scriptures themselves. There it expresses the Semitic view that the new does *not* replace the old but reveals the deepest dimensions and meanings of the old and causes the old to produce maximum yield. The maligned "old man" is finally given full justice and indeed may be called "new." Indeed, the final words of the New Testament (Rev. 21:1-8) would lose no weight were they to stand in the middle of the Old Scriptures. (In fact, they do stand there in Isaiah 65:17.)

We must, as Christians, remove an ingrained bias centered in the contrast between Old and New Scriptures. Better to work from the principle that the Old is not as old as it seems, and the New is not as new as our tradition has often portrayed it.

When ideas that are not recognizable within the context of the old faith are claimed to be new in the New Testament, it may be best to reserve judgment and, at least tentatively, to question whether those ideas are really in the New Testament at all. "Tentatively," because what the New Testament says does so often seem to come from the Old Scriptures. It remains an open question whether *everything* in the New comes from the Old Scriptures. But, let us at least create mental space to consider whether so-called "new ideas" don't look quite different the longer they are viewed in their literary and historical contexts.

What's this all leading to? A great deal has happened, and too little conversion has taken place—not only conversion of the heart, but also of the theological head. The main point cannot be whether everything jibes with a familiar (and not altogether dependable) book. The main point is that we need to free ourselves from the inherited burden which maintains a superficial climate categorized as "promise and fulfillment," for example. In such catch-alls, the content of the New Testament is made to justify artificial theological presumptions of which we should be ashamed.

Granite or *Midrash*

The expression "Scripture is the word of God" has been given a fixed place in the dogma that all Scripture is inspired. Our package of beliefs contains many more such formulas. Accepting this package "wholesale" and "sight unseen," however, does not necessarily comprise the "respect for tradition" that postmodern critiques of modernity's anti-traditionalism counsel. Rather, such uninspected but assumed packages of beliefs contain information that is accessible to everyone. But we need to keep our eyes open—even if it only means questioning the meaning of accepted dogmatic formulas. For, once "canonized"—even in the special sense of being "declared holy"—the formulas go on to lead a life of their own. With centuries of authority behind them, they run the risk of producing a self-deluded dream world that keeps us from our work.

So, bewildered or relieved, we come to the conclusion that the Old Scriptures are far from the block of granite that you would expect from the word of God. From all we now know from scholarship, including the history of their development, the Old Scriptures have many of the earmarks of coincidental, provisional, and questionable human utterance. To say it so plainly risks causing scandal but anyone who falls over that one has played hookey from school too often. Instead, spiritual adulthood requires that we accept insight into the vulnerable nature of "the way of the Lord" as the beginning of biblical ABC's.

Such insights make the biblical stories no less powerful, and certainly no less touching. They still move you. Isn't this the very thing that makes it the word of God? People are fallible when taken one by one, but somehow more reliable when their wisdom as a people over time is taken together. The dogma of "biblical inspiration," indeed, must be examined against the scriptural processes themselves rather than be taken as adequate in its present formulation. Otherwise this kind of dogmatic formula becomes a blind *a priori* that leads to pious and unconscious heresies that improperly claim for themselves a monopoly on orthodoxy.

When such claims arise, it's best to begin at the beginning, in yourself, because individual human life experiences are the source of scriptural witness. Looking with an open mind leads you to the heart-warming discovery that it's not so much an all-knowing One who lets people speak on God's behalf. Rather it is people who let their God speak and demonstrate what has become of their own laboriously conquered and transcended holy convictions and obligation.

There's a fine Jewish term for this. In order not to corrupt it at the offset we won't explain it right now. Instead, we'll gradually and reluctantly fill in the gaps. In fact, you discover that the Scripture is one big *midrash,* a pure *midrash* on the phenomenon called humanity.

We say *midrash* because this term, besides being right on the mark, is unpretentious and affords plenty of room for filling in the meaning. We use *midrash* especially in the sense that Scripture cannot be exhausted of its subject. It is not the last word. Rather, it is the first word that asks for and inspires new words from its own store. Scripture suggests only one possibility among seventy others, and those it leaves to us. Rightly so, because speaking of being human involves us no less than our Scripture-writing forebears. Seventy, the number of infinity (as in "forgive your brother seventy times seven"), is connected with the people and languages enumerated in Genesis 10. There is a Pentecostal miracle there that takes place around one Scripture.

The Growing Word

The Scriptures' motley makeup is striking, once one gets beyond our Bibles' stately bindings that trick us into thinking it is one book. Insight into how that motleyness goes hand in hand with a profound unity is something one learns only by the grace of patient attentiveness. Countless bits of information of every conceivable kind and origin, products of their place and time, are stored in the Scriptures. But all that unmanageable and intractable material is made subservient to a single great meaning. It becomes the means by which inspiration, comparable to artistic inspiration, was expressed, inspiration which consistently pressed its way into the most remote places and back streets.

The fortitude which prompts both preservation and synthetic understanding is obviously religious inspiration. In fact and by definition, inspiration provides no new data, but gradually digs deeper into the human data that is available. The faith tradition then takes place within the process by which people pass life on to each other, by word of mouth, from mother to daughter, from father to son.

During its thousand-year growth process, the Scripture is an accompanying phenomenon, a product—or byproduct—of a more or less united people who, in gradually widening relationships, pass on both what they've received and what they've experienced. In this way, the story expands from generation to generation. Its growth is extensive. And in the growth, more profile is added to a striking "collective personality." The story gains more and more "character." Its growth is *intensive* as well as *longitudinal.*

We watch the growth. One person's story becomes a family story, and it continues on from family to clan or tribe and to a people consisting of many tribes which begins to find its identity in a still-nomadic tribal alliance. When this alliance invades the region and begins to settle down (see Jos. 24 for the program), the folktale, with all the native material included, becomes the national story of the state in the vicissitudes of the two kingdoms during and after the monarchy. After national collapse, the national block of tradition doesn't go away. It is still visible and becomes the basis of the story which separates the world community from that of the exiles. Still further in the future, it preserves the exiled nation and helps create the Jewish community's self-understanding in the diaspora and the age of the second temple.

Word of Faith

The main line of the story reflects just as much the vicissitudes of Israel's neighbor and brother, Edom; cousins of shame—Moab and Ammon; blood relative Aram-

Damascus; and, in their way, Phoenicians and Philistines—as it reflects the creation of Israel itself in its odyssey from nomadic group to political state association to minority group in a world-girdling empire.

This procedure, determined by the balance of power among the great nations, makes very clear that the exceptional things professed in the Bible are not to be found in external events themselves—although the Bible continually and literally says so—but in the way in which people deal with these things. A profane or neutral story has become a story of faith.

No matter how silent or absent God seems to be, faith draws God into human events against all appearances. That is why it is faith. Herein lies the biblical way to teach the attitude of faithfulness. The story turns the hidden activity of God into observable events that took place in the past. The God of the Covenant appears, speaks, and intervenes. God promises and gives land, conducts the Israelites' wars, rejects the people and removes them from sight, and one day God will gather this people together from all the corners of the earth.

What does the Scripture, with its powerful stories, want us to believe? When do you believe in the Scriptures?

There is a *fundamentalist* way of understanding the Scriptures: you believe in the Scriptures when you believe that God did indeed do exactly what the Scriptures say. But in this fundamentalist approach, the confirmation of belief is out of alignment with the rest of what we know about history. The receiver has been set on the wrong wavelength and there is an immense waste of spiritual energy defending faith from the rest of human experience. It is exactly the sense of biblical faith that we have lost in arguments with moderns over historical minutiae, a process that endlessly discusses whether something "really happened." An overloaded fundamentalist faith continues the argument at the expense of what the disputed story really wants to teach.

By way of contrast, in the view proposed in this book, *you believe in the Scriptures when you allow them to convince you that your life has sense and purpose.* Earlier believers made that discovery with regard to their lives, and they want to make us partners in their belief through the medium of their spectacular stories. *We don't really believe their story until we extract from it the understanding that what the story recounts is happening right now, that it can happen, if we remain open to it and make the story our own.*

Salvation History

Israel's neighbors related their story with the same kinds of facts, but only in Israel were they given a divine common denominator in a unique way (how unique is to be filled in later)—even Moab's ups and downs depended on the favor or wrath of his god Chemosh (Judges 11:24). It is a story about people and "their" God, or, just as correctly, a story about God and God's people. Who these people must be, against all appearances, remains to be filled in later. Amos exposes what we take for granted:

> Are you not like the Ethiopians to me,
>   O people of Israel? says the Lord.
> Did I not bring up Israel from the land of
>   Egypt,
>   and the Philistines from Caphtor and the
> Syrians from Kir? (9:7)

Yet the Lord says in Isaiah: "Blessed be Egypt my people, and Assyria the work of my hands, and Israel my heritage" (19:25).

Both texts convey the idea that the only faith dimension is that which creates from a people a divinely chosen people and from their history a salvation history.

Creation is, then, a salvific act. To be human on this earth is a divine offer of salvation, a revelation. But this salvation and this revelation are realized only through human acceptance. Israel's yes and no are a national formulation of the human yes and no that is both universal and timeless.

This section hopes to convey the understanding that the troublesome aspects of the Scriptures experienced by many Bible readers (the national restriction and accompanying contrast between Israel and other nations) are determined by historic situations and concrete limitations intrinsic to history. They belong to the "material" of the Scriptures; they are, in other words, contingent biblical facts. The quotes mentioned earlier from Amos and Isaiah emphatically rid the air of any illusions in this regard. These facts, however, do have a bearing on thematic information in the completed Scriptures. These become a "theme of belief" which, with help from national material, takes on a plastic formulation (with an appeal to fantasy).

A "theme" of election, for instance, could be a point of orientation for persons standing at a crossroad in life or facing a choice. The two attitudes from which they must choose are the way that Israel is called to go and the way that the other nations are in the habit of going:

> You shall not do as they do in the land of Egypt [nor] in the land of Canaan . . . My ordinances you shall observe and my statutes you shall keep following: I am the Lord your God. You shall keep my statutes and my ordinances; by doing so one shall live. I am the Lord (Lev. 18:1-5).

The usage originally may have been nationalistic, but the contrast between Israel's God and the gods of the other nations mentioned in the Scriptures suggests a conflict that must be decided in every human heart. True faith confesses that the individual is drawn together in a covenant with an inviting God: you love me and follow my way by actively loving your neighbor.

New Humanity/New God

This God travels along with people, grows with them from "my God" and "God of my fathers" to family god and to a tribal and national god. Yahweh is the God of the covenant that the tribes draw up among themselves (and so with their God), swearing mutual allegiance with the God whose name, not accidentally, is a program of assistance.

Even the divine nomad becomes sedentary. The god of the tent becomes a god of the temple and finally a god of the state, until the godhead is discovered, better "revealed," as a god of the world of humanity. So "the God of our fathers" becomes "Everlasting Father, Prince of Peace," Messiah of the future ages in Isaiah 9:6.

God is not just a "god" but This God and no other. The essential question is "What kind of god?" The answer is the old and classic biblical theme—our God is the Only Real One, one who made a name, greater and greater, more and more filled with what is authentic and with what is asked of a person at the deepest level, until the name no longer fit anything that is naturally called "god"—idols made of and representing power—gold and silver, horses and chariots (Is. 2:7-8; Jer. 10:2-16).

In this story, though, "god" and "being human" (*Dasein*) are discovered and defined together. That is why a new situation for the people in the story means making a new, always different God, making every moment new. There is constant interaction. This God changes, renews people, makes their history. For after the Exile the history shared with other nations is over. Other nations fall away but Israel revives, is more than ever itself. Something must have been going on for a very long time. As Julius Wellhausen (d. 1918) once said, "Take Israel and Moab, two grains of seed like two indistinguishable drops of water. Yet they produced two totally different plants. That means that the seeds must have been essentially different."

New situations lead to a new God, to new Writings, to a new understanding of the Scriptures received in tradition. The path of development schematically described here, which God and humankind go through together, assumes profound changes and true revolutions in the pattern of God and society. Passing from one sociological structure to the other meant more than merely adding a chapter to the national heritage to describe the new experiences. It meant, instead, that under the influence of these experiences the old chapters were retold in entirely new ways.

In this way the material of a story, the grit of it, starting indeed as a very local tale, grows into the shape of "the Great-Israel Vision," finally sharing its character as a program of life, in short, as Torah. The nomadic story thus takes on the prospect of seizing the land and even of establishing a kingdom of Solomon-like allure. Yet throughout the process, Abraham keeps, in exemplary manner, commandments that arose a thousand years later (Gen. 18:19), and the exiles in Babylon tell their own story in the desert cycle.

In this fashion originates the Book called "Bible" in a last step on the way from plurality to unity, for in European languages, the word *Bible* comes from the Late Latin feminine singular *biblia* ("book"), but its roots lie ultimately in the Greek neuter plural *biblia* ("books").

Scriptural Inspiration

Now that the many books have become one Book there arises a need for one uniform notion of inspiration that is equally applicable to all the books of the Bible, no matter how divergent in character and quality, one that will distinguish them from all other books. What makes a book a holy book? How does a document become Holy Scripture? The Bible? Because for many years there was too little information available to give an answer rooted in sound history, scholars took a *theological* approach. First, one can observe that in the Bible there is a broad notion of inspiration through the spirit of God that can be applied to any human activity. A particular subset of that general notion of inspiration is designated when one refers to the development of a book—one can call it the "inspiration to write" or "scriptural inspiration."

Patristic and medieval disputes over what the prophetic charism alters in the prophet were, after the Council of Trent, applied to "the sacred writer." An attempt was then made to discover the way in which the writer's capacities and faculties were influenced or inspired by God, the "principal author," who was portrayed as enlisting people to write a kind of detailed letter from Heaven addressed to us. During protracted disputes over such matters, scriptural inspiration became almost independently pre-eminent. What resulted was a *theological formula* that came to be understood rigidly as a technically defined *historical fact*, something concrete. Over time, it became customary to present the reality of divine-human interaction in a straightforward, rectilinear way. But life is more than that, and new data was found that illuminated the complexity of Scriptures' origin (Copernicus/Galileo).

Almost exactly a century ago, a new source of excitement was born. Previous to that no one would doubt the truth that Tobiah's dog wagged his tail (Tobit 6:2) if the Bible said so, or that in the beginning was the word—exactly as the Scriptures said. For, when the entire body of Scripture is inspired and is *univocally* the word of God, I am obliged to believe that Tobiah's dog wagged his tail as much as the fact that the Word became flesh. Everyone, of course, had a feeling that such matters were not on the same plane, but there was no acceptable principle for coming to a new understanding. You heard it said that if we start to make distinctions between what we are required to believe in the Scriptures and what we don't have to believe, where will we end up?

In the end, the question was (and had to be), What does tradition actually mean with its deceptively clear language? How does that language correspond to history? Clarity was reached by putting scriptural inspiration back into the whole from which it had been artificially detached by theological vivisection.

Inspiration of Faith

The "light" of inspiration is in fact nothing other than the "light of faith," insofar as it can flow into a book. The book is like a coastline. It arises through a normal geological growth process and determines the shape of the sea, but in another sense the sea remains what it always was.

Scriptural inspiration is connected with the light of faith by which things are seen, evaluated and judged. These things can be lofty, but they can also be very ordinary. When you're dealing with the origin of scriptural material, it doesn't much matter if it has fallen from the sky or if it's a common observation, whether it's historically reliable or a folk legend. Scripture gives up the essence of its material without fanfare, just as it is. In its ordinariness lies its intrinsic value. Recording *this* material in the Scriptures does not elevate the ordinary beyond itself or grant certainty to the uncertain, let alone infallible certainty.

Therefore we can rest assured that the entire body of Scripture is inspired because this inspiration lays claim to all the scriptural ingredients, and each one, in its own way and its own place, contributes to Scripture's expression of faith.

So it is an abuse of Scripture when theologians pelt each other with bits of text as though they are so many words of God. We should, then, suspect that something is the word of God only because of the power of expression that all those words together convey. And we should be a bit more reverent in the way we talk about Jesus, rather than handling him as some kind of divine oracle of truth.

Our brother Paul writes occasional letters in haste in moments stolen from a busy schedule. They are emotional and up-to-the-minute, aided by a vocabulary and an arsenal of ideas that he, as a child of his times and education, had at his disposal. Thus he reveals his holy conviction, in a way that is sometimes long-winded, one-sided and polemical. He is a faith witness and even a "sacred writer," although he never pretended to be a writer of Holy Scriptures. How could he? He just wrote. And he once left a cloak behind in Troas (2 Tim. 4:13).

And so things went on, no differently than they do today, without supernatural interference. Life just goes on. Things happened first and foremost from the bottom up. Only when the human portion is assessed and honored can we see whether there's anything left for God to do. If it's right, there won't be anything left over, because by definition God doesn't *add* anything to human existence; instead God *bears* it, *penetrates* it and, wherever people are open, God truly *comes*. God's presence is discovered. In short, inspiration does exactly what it says. It inspires, it takes whatever is on hand and "charges" it, fills it with energy, according to the nature of the thing.

And so the Scripture, and all that's in it, is a work of the Spirit because in its final form it is the work of people who mobilize all that's in them in order to pass on their conviction.

Inspiration—Now or Never

Nevertheless, we remain much too saddled with a book that is a kind of miracle wrought in the past during that privileged time (*in illo tempore*) when miracles occurred as a matter of course, all of which, according to one theological formula, ended with the close of the New Testament canon. There is, of course, a pious patristic explanation for this. According to that explanation, the early community was like a newly planted tree that required enormous amounts of water. But once it was well-rooted it could be left to itself and to the normal course of nature.

This family of assumptions is still with us, leading us to believe that scriptural inspiration is an exceptional activity of the Spirit, limited to particular people at a particular time. Indeed, the aim was the creation of the Book whose authoritative "holiness" ("set-apartness") was defined for all time. Once that book existed, the activity of the Spirit could cease with the death of the last prophet (Malachi), according to Jewish theory, or with the death of the last apostle, according to Christian theory, because then "revelation" could be limited. The "deposit of faith" (*depositum fidei*) was completed, and nothing new could be added. Everything that followed would be explanation and disclosure and confined to the competence of specially ordained authorities.

This is not nonsense in itself, but it can become nonsense if we swallow it whole. It is, contrariwise, a sign of a sound notion of the dynamics of faith to pose the questions, Why then and not now? Why there and nowhere else?

The local tastes and temporal flavors of the sacred books are only indigestible when *a priori* restrictive notions are imposed upon the Scriptures and make readers believe the Bible must be uniform because inspired by one God. Such *a priori* constructs, however, fail to take into account concrete historical situations, which impose limitations on individual stories in the Scriptures, Old and New. In addition, we need to recognize that these limitations lead us to concentrate on phenomena which occurred in the past at stipulated times, forgetting that, in principle, they can occur anywhere and at any time.

Under regnant popular notions of inspiration and revelation, the completed book—even though there is often no consensus as to when it was completed—delineates a certain sphere of influence of the Spirit as privileged, even though the same Spirit, which blows where it will and wherever people open themselves through faith, is wherever inspiration happens.

The Bible grew out of faithful living. From what we can know historically (that is to say, "on the basis of demonstrable evidence"), what was preserved happened in some measure by chance, and the Book came to an end at a roughly definable time. But the end need not have occurred then, and the life of faith goes on without any necessary or definable frontier to divide biblical from post-biblical experience. In an actual extension of the Scriptures, faith produces a stream of post-biblical literature from which, for the first thousand years, new "gathering places" for faith-expression arose, much as occurred in classic Talmudic literature and is seen in Migné's collection of the writings on the Greek and Latin Church Fathers, just to name two examples.

Naturally, the chain of events leading to the canon cannot be turned around. It began with the Scriptures, which contain our oldest, irreplaceable family papers, and the collection of the earliest strata influences all the traditions that follow it. Still, this is probably the most notable thing that can be said about Scripture's primacy and privileged position.

Scripture and its inspiration are, then, largely misunderstood by people who miss the point concerning why Scripture originated and who seem to fear that a more accurate view of Scripture will somehow diminish a need to believe in the uninterrupted religious progress or compromise a sense of the eternal nearness of God. But Scripture's intention is to make these very things visible in their familiar way of occurring: *Scripture tells of past "revelatory" events, events that also happen all through human history, including present day history; and Scripture does so because it wants to disclose the faith dimension intrinsic to all human history.*

Origin as Key to Understanding

The faith charism which the Scriptures brought into being is, therefore, ours as well. Our faith community is writing a new chapter in the history of faith. It won't be recorded in the canonical Scriptures, but in their light we can re-read and "re-write" the Scriptures—indeed, we can "write our own Bible." Both giving birth to the Scriptures *in illo tempore* ("in that [primordial] time") and understanding the Scriptures *in nostro tempore* ("in our own time") are fruits of the same charism. There's just as much talent necessary for producing the original work as in a truly creative "re-presentation."

The birth of the Scriptures follows a clear, recognizable line here. Whenever we follow and trace that line we are on the safe track toward mature scriptural understanding. The phases of the growth of the Scriptures that we can now identify through scholarship reveal that our forebears passed the Scriptures from hand to hand, writing and re-writing them in the light of ongoing history.

The identification of these phases in the composition of the Scriptures, enriched by the ability to select available related non-biblical materials, makes it possible for us to re-produce the art forms of our fathers. With insight into what they did, we have license to treat "their" Scriptures in such a way that they truly become "our" Scriptures—not merely as a book recording their faith, but equally as the book of our faith.

New situations arise in ongoing history. Some may even be unprecedented situations. They no longer lead to the writing of new canonical Scriptures. It is sufficient that they lead to a new understanding of the Scriptures.

That happens when the incidents related in the Scriptures are understood as expressions of timeless human language which demand, beg, and cry out that we interpret with eyes of faith what is happening today in our own world.

Part 2 | THE COURSE AND DEVELOPMENT OF THE WORD

2 | The National Period
1000 - 750 BCE
Jahwist and Elohist Sources

Portraying Origins "in days of old"

From the nature of the Scripture as a book of faith, it follows that Scripture's origin coincides in one way or another with the mysterious origin of the religious tradition to which it stands as its oldest document.

To ask about the origin of a book is to ask where and when the data that are processed into the book began to accumulate. It means in particular to ask where and when originated the vision of life's meaning and direction that combines all that data into the tightly composed whole we see in today's Bible.

The literal content of the Scriptures, that is, biblical history, has a unequivocal answer to that question. The Mosaic Covenant in the Sinai Desert is a new beginning that was solemnly celebrated with a founding charter in the Book of Exodus. Yet, despite this Covenant's apparent antiquity, it has a more ancient prototype, a begin-

ning that points to an earlier initiative, summarized in
the Covenant with Abraham (Gen. 18:18). Eventually,
the managing editors of the Scriptures attempted to
extend the line of belief back to the absolute beginning
via the Covenant with Noah (Gen. 9:9), which somehow
led back further to the "Adamic" Covenant (Gen. 1:26-
31), portrayed as the original Covenant.

Regardless of how important inquiry into the origins
of the history of the Covenant is, it is not of prime
interest here. It is an indisputable fact that all these
covenants are constructed from later material, namely,
from Israel's later experiences and ritual practices.

Thus the Covenant with Abraham recounted in Genesis 15:18 (compare Ex. 23:31), in which a piece of land
the size of Solomon's kingdom is the main issue, is taken
up again in Genesis 17 and made into a covenant of
circumcision because this, like the Sabbath Covenant
(Ex. 31:12-17), after the Exile had become a pillar of a
new, only now distinctly "Jewish," religious way of life.

That is the usual biblical way to deal with history. The
story of an irretrievable or barely retrievable beginning
can be retold in as broad a way as possible because it is
overlaid with the texture of subsequent events for which
it acts as legitimation, interpretation, or practical
norm—in short, *as Torah*.

Not merely by means of verbal pronouncements or
propositions but through all its historical contours and
layers, Scripture provides information about a growth
process in which the faith community develops an ever
more striking identity. In accomplishing its theological

goals, the retold story gives the impression that later material was already extant when the earlier event occurred. That's the impression it wants to give, for the sake of recognizability, but in giving it, later editions of the story deal with history in ways far different from contemporary rules for using historical materials permit.

Thus Abraham, not as a *historical* but as a *biblical* figure, is the exemplary father of the faith for all succeeding generations of Israelites, each major period introducing something of its own character into Abraham's portrait. In this way, the whole biblical narrative rests on a continuous and impressive anachronism. In this way, too, Scriptures use mainly the "form" or "image" of earlier individuals, while the content of the stories told, in fact, reflects the people of a subsequent generation to whom they are addressed.

The Desert Heritage

In inquiries about the beginning of Israel's faith, we must say, on the one hand, that the stories of Abraham and Sinai are already fruits of that faith and not mere statements of historical fact. Israel, for instance, probably emerged from *within* Canaanite culture, at least in part, and was not primarily an alien invasion, as the Bible portrays it. In terms of historical accuracy, it is also necessary to note that the tribes that are portrayed as settling in Canaan after 1200 already have such a pronounced Israelite religious character that they are not assimilated into Canaanite cultural patterns. Instead, they utilize the Canaanite heritage to accomplish their own goals. The constant and growing identity of Israel, present on every page of the Bible, reveals itself as a "desert" acquisition.

The part of the ancient world known as the Fertile Crescent, with its centers of power and culture, is full of people and gods. It is an established and sacred world. The desert, however, is no-man's-land. It belongs neither to a god nor is it subjugated by civilized groups. Thus a group of people living there—a group of runaway slaves, for instance—would have to take pains if they were to survive. They would be dependent on one another. They would discover and unveil a core of existence, naked facts, stripped of any obscuring interpretation. They would develop a sensitivity (so characteristic of the Bible) for the real and the authentic, for what really matters—making sure, for instance, that the brother next to you stays on his feet during a brutal journey (Lev. 25:35-36; Dt. 15:7-8, 11). Such events make empty hearts full (Ex. 15:1-19). Such concern makes bitter water sweet (Ex. 15:22-27), and it makes mere human beings into truly humane persons.

Whoever has tasted deeply this kind of humanity no longer hungers after other gods and is forever liberated from every preconceived view of the nature of "heaven." The desert wanderers are liberated from Egypt and its gods (Ex. 12:12) and—wrestling with stubborn earthly facts—they discover the nameless and non-localizable

God whose word and being are at once program and exemplar of the human task ahead.

Along their wanderings they come across the divine Name—"I am who I am" (Ex. 3:13-15)—which is understood associatively as expressing precisely what has become their deepest conviction. The Name liberates and opens them as a people for the future; it formulates what this people should and can be for one another. Whenever this happens, the Name is "sanctified" or "hallowed." That Name is proclaimed by a simple ark, a portable cultic object that keeps the program of the Name alive and accompanies the people on "all their journeys." From that day forward, it is their distinguishing feature that they "wander" in the Name of that God (Mic. 4:5).

The faith began at some point in time and took on its own features in the desert. And through all the ages, by virtue of its rich matrix, it will continue to be found in human desert experiences. These experiences are marked and recognizable in the biblical desert cycle, composed as this is by the later exiles who, after all, are eternal desert wanderers.

The desert continues to be the assigned and privileged place where God, over and over again, is given realistic, human shape. In the desert of history, God is revealed to the people: "the God of the Hebrews has met with us" (Ex. 3:18; 5:3). The situation in the desert is where the living God can be found and "the day of the assembly" (Dt. 9:10; 10:4; Hos. 12:10) celebrated through the ages in the "today" of Covenant liturgy (Ps. 95:7).

Keeping these observations in mind, imagine for a moment the course of events. Undoubtedly, all kinds of group traditions for various individual and communal events—births, burials, marriages, journeys, disputes and agreements about wells and pastures, and so forth— came together as a coherent whole as Covenant celebrations developed. These functioned both as social and liturgical events. They reinforced group identity in the presence of the Name. The high point of these Covenant celebrations, ideally if not actually, was the renewal of the famous Covenant of the Twelve Tribes portrayed in Deuteronomy.

There is, then, a demonstrable point where a more or less formulated interpretation of this heritage might grow, a place for a sort of national literature-in-the-making, a phenomenon accompanying a tribal alliance that is itself a transition in the development "from people to state." What this tribal Covenant heritage contains can be concluded from what the scribes do with this oral legacy.

National Unification

Setting aside the common notion that great literature is "beautiful writing," it can justifiably be said that the Old Scriptures began as a "national literature" of a particular people. The problem of national unification, however, would only be settled after the year 1,000 BCE with the foundation of the unified kingdom of David and of the first son of David, actually a personal union of the two kingdoms of Israel and Judah (2 Sam. 2:4 and 5:3-5).

In addition to the group name of the northern tribes under the leadership of "the house of Joseph" (Ps. 80:2) and in addition to the name of the later Northern Kingdom (also called Ephraim), Israel is also the collective name for the land as a whole. The twelve tribes are represented by the twelve sons of Jacob, also known as Israel (Gen. 32:28 and 35:10; Ex. 24:4; 1 Kg. 18:31 and 2 Kg. 17:34).

David completes the conquest of the land. Under him, the four ancient enclaves (around Hebron, Shechem, Galilee, and Transjordania) become one united geographic region. This resulted, ethnically speaking, in a hodge-podge that was more probably unified under the state covenant than under the religious covenant. This pluralistic indigenous element finds an enduring center in the capital cities of Jerusalem and Samaria.

David's politics were aimed at making his city into a national capital and his court chapel into a national sanctuary. The translation of the ark, so closely bound up with the Name of the God of the Covenant, means that the cult of Yahweh ("Yahwehism") becomes the state religion. In retrospect, this can be seen as a prelude to the monopoly on worship later claimed by Jerusalem, which is emphasized so strongly in various biblical strata (see Ps. 78:67-70; Dt. 12; Lev. 17; Jos. 22). A whole theology grew up based on the sin of Jeroboam, who dared to construct an alternative site for worship (1 Kg. 12:28 and Ex. 32:4; 1 Kg. 13; 2 Kg. 17; 2 Chr. 13:4-12; 30:5-9).

The process of adapting nomadic Israelite desert faith patterns to residential (Canaanite) cultural conditions that had begun much earlier continued in full swing under the kings. For example, the agrarian festal calendar and the indigenous language, later to be known as "Hebrew" but now still called "the language of Canaan" (Is. 19:18) and "Judean" (2 Kg. 18:26) were adopted.

A Thousand Years

During the early monarchy (David and Solomon, approximately 1000-925 BCE), Israel reaches the average standard of contemporary culture and learns to adapt the former oriental culture as an expression of its own character and essence. This means that Israel begins writing and that the written tradition begins supporting or even taking precedence over the task of orally transmitting the faith tradition.

To get an overview of millennium of writing activity, we'll divide the period into four sections of 250 years each. At the same time, we'll work in the classic, four-source documentary strata hypothesis, originally proposed about 1900. For convenience we shall use the usual four letters to indicate the four sources: "J" (for Yahwistic), "E" (for Elohistic), "D" (for Deuteronomic), and "P" (for the Priestly Code). Although this theory has weaknesses, it rests on a careful inventory and classification of literary and theological scriptural factors that, despite their problems, continue to benefit contemporary exegesis.

The principal phases of literary production, brought to light by Pentateuch research, are equally recognizable in the rest of the Old Scriptures. When used loosely, these symbols (J, E, D, and P) can be used also to denote the phases in which the entire body of Scripture develops.

New Stories

The main elements of the Pentateuchal (first five books) or the Hexateuchal (first six books) period are no longer objects of exclusively oral tradition, as they were previously when the narrative grew into individual stories or groups of stories. More and more frequently, a "writer" is the main creator of the story. The purest example of this is the story in which David's succession is the main subject (2 Sam. 9-20 and 1 Kg. 1-2), perfect examples of the storyteller's art. From this same period also comes the first written version of stories of David's youth and stories about Samuel and Saul, which can be understood only by recalling that an earlier oral process left many traces behind. These traces still play a main role in the heroic sagas of Gideon and Samson and in the stories of the lives of Elijah and Elisha, all told within the community of the "prophets' sons."

These and similar stories are still part of the national period, as is evident from the way they retain the flavor of the by-gone period of the kings. They have been collected into complete written units, but only in the following period will they be brought into the greater whole of particular biblical books.

It is the nature of the tradition process that literary activity has a double task to perform. First, it must carry forward to posterity relevant and still accessible contemporary information while adding to it the group's already appropriated heritage. The outline traced above gives at least a skeletal impression of how that occurred during this period.

New Synthesis from Old Material

Tradition's second task is to pass on the already existing heritage, not as a dead block, however, but as a witness that can be brought to life by unique individual experiences in ongoing history. Thus we can thank this period (1000 to 925 BCE) for creating the first written synthesis of the entire Israelite heritage that had been passed down, mostly on an oral basis, and that had survived for many generations.

When contemporary experiences are being passed on in writing, naturally the oral legacy that was accumulated up to that time must also be handed down. Writing is a new modern medium which has to be adapted to the entire tradition. In this synthesis, the contents of the basic structure (the main narrative) and the material of the story of the first six books of the Bible (the Hexateuch) are essentially all present.

Each tradition goes from synthesis to synthesis. Often dominant personalities play a decisive linking and identifying function. In such figures as Moses and David, for instance, the past coalesces, thus paving a way toward the future. These heroes' influence keeps on working. A synthesis like this is reached first in the concrete process of corporate life itself. Once it's there, it leaves a mark on literary production, which, in its turn, becomes a synthetic factor in the creation of the community's growing self-understanding. This comprises the well-known relationship between a national character, on the one hand, and every classic national literature, on the other.

This exchange applies to a great extent to the Scriptures. A group of people brings a book into being, and then the book becomes an important factor in shaping the people's future and keeping them going as a people. This, in fact, is what occurs in each of the periods we are commenting on in this sketch.

The written synthesis described here can also be regarded as both the literary reflection of and as the result of the national unification under David and Solomon. Groups of stories such as those mentioned earlier are characteristic of this unification.

Yahwist and Elohist

Indeed, this synthesis is so strongly related, both literarily and theologically, to the biography of David that it must also have arisen within the environment of Judah and Jerusalem. Because the frequent use of the four-letter Name (J-H-W-H, the Tetragrammaton) was first noted at the beginning of modern scientific research, "The Yahwist" is the accepted, if not tactful, name for this oldest layer in the stratification of our Bible.

Bringing the Ark of the Covenant to Jerusalem (with all the tribal tradition attached to it) underscores the national unification and explains the Yahwist signature on the literary synthesis flowing from that event. In the simple reference to the J story or the J tradition, the letter J can also recall both the name of God and Judah/Jerusalem.

The same unscientific freedom can be taken with respect to the letter E, used for the sake of brevity in references to the E tradition. This is based on the predominant use of the divine name Elohim (i.e., god or gods or divine creatures—"sons" of God). The background of the Elohist story is found in the Northern Kingdom, also called Ephraim, and it shows traces of early prophetic influence, possibly connected with the appearance there of Elijah and Elisha, which makes four E's.

During the Monarchy there arises a synthetic national vision which, after the split of the Kingdom in 925, is carried on in the Southern and Northern Kingdoms. The J story (around 900) may be seen as the written establishment of that vision in southern circles. Around 800, the northern version of the same communal vision was set in writing (the E story). But this can all be forgotten when one considers that in the Bible only a synthesis of J plus E (around 700) survives.

The Ancient Period

This J + E synthesis is itself a reflection of what first took place among living people. Around the time of the fall of Samaria in 722 BCE, groups of northerners, faithful people, emigrated to the Southern Kingdom. They brought their heritage with them. The requirements of the times forced these people to gather around their common religious property and led to a new literary synthesis. Because this took place in the Southern Kingdom, the J story is its foundation, filled in here and there with what was or appeared to be the immigrants' material from the E tradition.

This makes for unavoidable duplicated passages ("doublets"). Indeed, whenever the same incident was transmitted for a considerable period of time in two distinct circles, two versions arose, which can give the impression that they record different facts. Thus we have Genesis 12:10-20 which should be compared with Genesis 20:1-18. Exodus 19 and 24 work from an E pattern, while Exodus 34 models a J pattern; and both patterns refer to the same liturgical praxis—celebrating the Covenant, which still retains its identifying origins in the desert!

It is pointless and impossible to unravel the two versions, because they can seldom stand alone. Still, it is useful to distinguish them, if the Bible reader has any notion of this sort of thing, because there are stories (J) with a spontaneous and rough character in which the Lord himself appears and speaks directly to people (Gen. 2-4) alongside other stories (E) that exhibit tendencies toward moralizing speculation, in which the Lord is involved by means of dreams, visions (see these elements in Gen. 15), and prophecies.

Then, to complicate things further, it sometimes appears as though the Deuteronomist begins to speak. It's more accurate, of course, to talk about pre-Deuteronomic elements at this juncture rather than about later Deuteronomic interpolations (Ex. 19:3-6; 22:21-24 or 20-23; 23:20-33 compared with Dt. 7). This occurs because the style of Deuteronomy only grew gradually. It had a pre-history that has left traces in earlier materials.

In practice, the J + E synthesis is best handled as one whole, composed in the period of national history, which is clearly recognizable in these strata of the Scriptures like a monumental city center. Subsequent generations may build new quarters in the city, each in its own characteristic style. And these styles will be recognized here and there in the old city center, which still retains its original character and atmosphere intact, despite the influence of later developments.

Consequently, we see in this national period two things happening which will keep on happening in the future: (1) the production of new literature (the expansion of Scripture); and (2) the retrieval (creative revival) of existing literature, oral and written (the renewal of Scripture).

Thus what resembles on the surface a biography of David (and similar passages) passes for new *production*. The synthesis of the heritage is, though, a creative *retrieval* of a national epic already in circulation—exodus, wandering in the desert, entry into the land—to which is added as prologue the story of the creation of humanity and the history of the patriarchs.

3 | The Prophetic Movement
750-500 BCE
Deuteronomist Source

Early Prophecy

The next period begins with a kind of prophesying portrayed in histories of Israel in the new land, stories or prophecy that strike one as primitive. We get such an impression of primitiveness from the stories about Elijah and Elisha, and about Samuel and Saul, for example. The way in which later traditions may have realized that the title *prophet* was projected backward upon earlier traditions is shown in the saying, "Is Saul also among the prophets?" (1 Sam. 10:11-12; 19:24).

The name *prophet*, we can confidently say, came to be applied to persons with a special talent for what is called prophesying, a term denoting the activities of those who enter an ecstatic state characterized by dancing and jumping, shouting and singing. In addition, the state can be provoked by carrying on such activities. Finally, prophecy seems to have involved certain professional, perhaps shamanlike techniques (as indicated in 1 Kings 18:26-29; 2 Kings 3:15).

This kind of prophesying doubtlessly had roots in the indigenous cultural patterns that agricultural Israel adapted to its own religious understandings. Thus, if Baal had a prophet—or a hundred prophets—the God of the Covenant must have them, too. Perhaps in the encounter between traditions some prophets even changed gods, as shown in Judges 6:25-32.

This kind of primitive prophesying was a fact of life in Israelite society before the Exile. Prophets, who could be recognized by their cloaks of animal hair and their leather girdles, roamed around in groups. They belonged to the class of prophets ("sons" of prophets) and formed a kind of guild whose leader was addressed as "Lord" or "Father." Some prophets were given jobs at court or in the sanctuary; others opened a private practice. One sometimes had to travel a great distance to consult with a prophet, especially on holy days (2 Kings 4:22-23).

Prophets represented a specific kind of social group, one as distinct and identifiable as priests, elders, and wise men (Jer. 18:18; Ezek. 7:26). Moreover, they were an integral part of society and one of the organs of the general religious-social decay. Thus, in effect, the Lord of hosts is saying: Do not listen to the words of the prophets who prophesy to you; they are deluding you. They speak visions of their own minds, not from the mouth of the Lord . . . Alas for the senseless prophets . . . your prophets have been like jackals among ruins (cf. Jer. 23:16; Ezek. 13:3).

The prophets became hacks, false prophets. "You shall serve as my mouth. They [your hearers] will turn to you, not you who will turn to them" (Jer. 15:19).

Classical Prophecy

In contrast to early prophecy is the "classical" prophecy of the "scriptural prophets," so named because many collections of their oracles have been preserved in the Scriptures.

The figures of Elijah and Elisha delineate a transition in prophecy. On the one hand, they were central figures in the old prophecy business. On the other hand, they unmistakably announced the voice of the God of the Covenant, although mainly through their deeds rather than their words. Classical prophecy is all voice. The ecstatic dimension was replaced by a clearly felt duty to receive and transmit the word of God.

Amos underscored this new approach by emphatically saying that he was not a prophet (7:14; Mic. 3:8). His conviction was too deep for that, too personal, too founded in facts. The facts were clear to him and led to a true discovery of the God of the Covenant—a meeting with God—perhaps gradually, perhaps in the blink of an eye. The prophetic vocation story, usually intended as a sermon, can also be a moving reflection on an entire life of prophetic toil, an extreme effort, a last will and testament.

The word of God was an announcement of calamity

born of the struggle to change the old, not-yet-collapsed national society into a living sign of the divine presence, which could only be done through justice and righteousness. The God of the Covenant had been manipulated, the same way that Baal (who had no real contact with everyday human conduct) had been. God had been reduced to a national label, to folklore, to a God whom people could dismiss with a few obligatory sacrifices (Ps. 50).

These new prophets had limited impact, however. Religious structures did not change, because those in the establishment were only concerned with their positions of power. Even so, the word did its work among the nameless group of people who were "quiet in the land" (Ps. 35:20). From this group it created the believers, the Lord's reserved seven thousand: "all the knees that had not bowed to Baal, and every mouth that had not kissed him" (1 Kings 19:18; Rom. 11:4). These few were "the rest," a "poor remainder" for the time being, predestined to become the Holy Remnant and seed of a new future. The prophecy of salvation was aimed at them.

Collection of Oracles

Around 750 BCE, the "scriptural prophets" made their appearance: Hosea and Amos in the Northern Kingdom, Isaiah and Micah in the Southern Kingdom. Together with their "major" (Jeremiah and Ezekiel) and "minor" successors ("the twelve" in one scroll, the

"Dodekapropheton"), the words of these "late" prophets did not receive canonical form until the next period.

We still are finding loose oracles, the smallest of units, appearing here and there like erratic boulders or flying leaflets (Isa. 2:2-4 = Mic. 4:1-3). Mostly we find them in blocks, series, or triplets, as if related oracles were attracted to one another according to their language or theme. In this way, larger units were born, organized according to a like-goes-with-like principle. Searching for mnemonic devices, the oral tradition tended to form collections that, even in their written form, ran from smaller to larger. Compare, in the synoptic gospels, the grouped pronouncements (*logia*) and parables.

As an example, Isaiah 1-12, which was put together from more or less intact fragments, is a symphonic composition. Within it, chapters 2-5 and 7-11 are large collections that had led independent lives. These collections themselves came into existence through mini-collections that grew together. Chapter 1, no matter how composed it may be, forms a living whole, a prologue with just the right text in the right place. Chapter 6 is easily understood as an independent vocation story but, placed in the middle, it has a many-sided linking function, pointing to the source of inspiration that grants authority to the material coming before and after it. Chapter 12 is again independent (a psalm of thanks), but in this location it works as a grand finale that reinforces the coherence of the previous eleven chapters.

Similarly, the first new contribution from this period provided a large supply of texts that are quite varied as far as contents and structure, since for every particular type of text there is a particular (conventional) type of style (literary genre). Each of the following types of text has its own pattern—symbolic reports, parables, satires, elegies, proverbs, disputes, lawsuits, prophetic Torah, threats ("Woe!"), messages, and so forth.

All these texts go back in groups to the appearance of striking personalities who had their own style, their own theology, and their own favorite themes. Their names live on in the biblical books named after them.

This enumeration evokes the image of an extensive land over which stacks of material lay dispersed here and there, or of a spectacular building complex covered in scaffolding, its electrical and plumbing lines still under construction. Many more lines remain to be extended, many more connections have to be put into place before the work is done.

There is already so much in these prophetic books because the text material is so explosive, has such vitality, and is ready and able to absorb new material within its fields of inspiration.

The Deuteronomist

A second new contribution is the continuation of the national story, beginning where the J story left off (or rather was broken off by the later marking out of the Pentateuch).

This prophetic story contains the early prophets,

Joshua, Judges, Samuel, and Kings. The stories and story groups worked into these texts date mostly from the previous period. Further along, we often come across information from the temple archives and the annals of the palace.

All this material was recorded in the context of and strung together with admonishing and evaluating preaching, a characteristic of the Book of Deuteronomy. This book works as an impressive prologue to the whole "deuteronomic history work" (the D story, around 500), right across the border of the Pentateuch.

A few examples of deuteronomistic editing include Deuteronomy 1-4:43 and 29-34 (setting of an older and shorter version of the book); Joshua 1 and 23 (theological framework for the story of the conquest and division of the land); Judges 2:6-22 (rhythm of history). Examples of evaluation include 1 Kings 14:22-24; 15:3-5, 11, 26, 34; 2 Kings 14:24-27; 17:7-23.

Deuteronomy

Now we come to a third and very special contribution, the Book of Deuteronomy itself, the center of the Old Scriptures, pivot, link, bridge (with traffic going in both directions) between the Torah and the Prophecy.

Deuteronomy is a glorious example of creative reproduction. It "revives" the first great chapter of the period of national tradition (story plus parties to the law) in a very synthesizing way. Moses himself tells the story, declares the laws, and makes his appearance as the mediator of the Covenant. This all takes place on the plains of Moab across the Jordan River from Canaan.

The format of the book is that of a covenantal liturgy: historical prologue, the main commandment, particular commandments, call to conversion, solemn consent, final curse and blessing.

The name Deuteronomy (meaning "second law") is a symbol for the book because it "repeats" the raw material of the synthesis brought about during the previous period, since that synthesis is now worked into the three central books of the Pentateuch (Exodus, Leviticus, and Numbers). It is not really important that the name refers to a faulty Greek translation of Deuteronomy 17:18 and Joshua 8:32, where a copy or duplicate of this law is mentioned.

The phrase "this law" (Deut. 17:18) alludes to an earlier, second-to-last version (Deut. 4:44-28:69, or 29:1). This version is constructed as follows. The strict code of the law is central (12-26). It is almost exclusively a collection of "particular commandments" (so called because they regulate human relationships), preceded by a "historical prologue" (4:44-11:32) in which the "main commandment" (the relationship with the God of the Covenant) plays a main role: the love of the Lord is realized through the observance of the codex (= the love of one's neighbor. See 1 John 4:21). A blessing and a curse form the final part of the text (27 and 28).

As far as the penetrative tone used in proclaiming the law and the parties to the law, the legal codex is based mainly on a tradition formed in the national tribal sanctuaries of the Northern Kingdom. In any case, the book is the result of a long tradition of preaching.

The codex may be regarded as a revised and augmented publication of the "Covenant book" (Exod. 20:22-23:33) that must have served as the charter in the liturgy of the old (prenational) tribal alliance. The center of this alliance lay in the north until David's time. Joshua 24 takes place in Shechem, a name avoided in the Greek Bible as a dirty word and replaced by Shiloh (Sir. 50:26). In fact, Shechem had been the central sanctuary for quite some time (Judg. 21:19; 1 Sam. 1:3; Jer. 7:12). It also occurs to us that the E tradition is northern and exhibits predeuteronomic traces.

The Book Is Discovered

The following depiction of events is quite plausible. In 722 BCE, the Northern Kingdom met its final disaster: the Assyrian exile. We are sure that groups of faithful people—particularly a large number of priests who had previously served the Torah in local temples—emigrated to the south.

This caused a problem. Deuteronomy 18:6-8 gives the northern viewpoint and demands that these northern priests be granted the same rights as the temple clergy. The Jerusalem viewpoint, which can be found in 2 Kings 23:9, is given harshly. The northern priests may return to work, but only in subordinate functions, and "they shall not come near to me, to serve me as priest, nor come near any of my sacred . . . things" because they are priests of idols who committed atrocities (Ezek. 44:10-16). This decision is cold and angry, showing clearly that certain fanatics had gotten their way. The text used to support this decision probably already had an anti-Samaritan flavor (as did 2 Kings 17:24-41); it certainly is fiercely anti-northern.

The one altar—that of Jerusalem—became a *theological* theme in the Scriptures. To read this as though the Bible takes sides in a historical and clerical conflict is a misreading. By no means does Scripture approve of a sacred centralism trying to make its power monopoly unassailable through a theological ideology in which people who are thoroughly in their own right (see 1 Kings 11:29-31, 35-38) become stigmatized as non-orthodox schismatic idolaters.

The northern priests were thus left to their own devices in a disinterested Jerusalem that continued to live its carefree life. Deuteronomy must have taken shape within this isolated circle. Reflections on their totally dislocated life, especially on the vexing question of how it could have come so far, led these priests to a profound change and to putting their own beloved traditions into writing. This is quite understandable, because the cult in which their oral tradition had its own fixed place no longer existed.

It's obvious that the self-assured temple clergy were not even able to muster up any ecumenical attention for this group. Such a situation leaves plenty of room for a discovery and for the finding of the book of the law or the book of the Covenant in the temple archives around the year 625 BCE (2 Kings 22-23).

Once discovered, this book becomes the Magna Charta of Judaism-in-birth trauma, a document that functions both as a book and as Scripture. The book becomes captivating afterwards, when the Southern Kingdom feels threatened with a similar catastrophe, and even more so when the oncoming calamity is an accomplished fact. Deuteronomy is doomed to remain contemporary as long as there are displaced persons whose whole existence has fallen to pieces.

The Program of the Second Desert Journey

The old sources, tapped anew, show the desert as the place of education and training for social sensibility (Deut. 8:5; Hos. 2:14-16), and prophetic belief was able to survive a total uprooting. In this new collective desert experience, belief cleared a path for the people, showing them their previously unused potential. In the long run, it gave them a new design for life.

A remnant people from the north first reached a synthesis through its daily wrestling with life. This synthesis was reflected in the social upheaval of Deuteronomy, which, in turn, helped gather Israel's scattered remnants into one faith community.

This situation—from now on the "Jewish" situation—was completely new. The new circumstances compelled people to revise their lives, to rethink and reformulate what had become accepted and trusted practice through centuries of life together as a nation, but which had also become threadbare and hollow: the entire complex of household effects comprising ideas and practices that people took for granted.

From the history of Israel's neighbors, who are also their partners in fate, it appears that even compelling circumstances do not automatically lead to real renewal. The outer situation never has the last word. It all comes down to people and their attitude.

The Role of Prophecy

What is unique about Israel is that its catastrophe is accompanied by a voice, the voice of the prophets. In retrospect, it's easy to see what prophecy was called to do. It detached the real values of the national past from its decadent government, so the religious attitude distanced itself from the state and its institutions, made itself independent, and learned to stand on its own two feet.

When Moab went down, it dragged its god Chemosh down with it. The collapse of Israel's government, however, liberated Israel's God and belief in God from the oppressive structures that had been suffocating belief.

The prophetic voice continued to make itself heard, in order to transplant the faith in new soil—faith that had returned to its naked core and been purified. This was necessary so that faith could take on a new form of adapted, pliable, subservient structures with a maximum of content and a minimum of apparatus.

Israel's most precious and unique possession—its human religious identity—survived the catastrophe undamaged, even strengthened. The Old Scriptures, more and more becoming a document, reached their high point. Israel's remnant found its deepest identity and put it into words in an irreplaceable and imperishable way.

The prophetic phenomenon is once and for all delineated in the figures of Moses (Deut. 18:15-19) and Samuel (1 Sam. 3:1; 9:9) with thematic links in Elijah and (in the biographical notes in Isaiah 8) Jeremiah and Ezekiel. In the heart of the Exile, all these prophetic features flowed together into the human reality of the Suffering Servant. Thanks to the moving songs of the disciples and eye-witnesses, the Servant's brief existence acquired all its meaning as liberating profile and program. The Old Scriptures are never as new as here, although one needs to note that Christian readings of the Servant motif as messianic, for instance, diverge from Jewish readings and may be bitterly rejected by Jews.

The Servant: Messiah of the Exiles

He is anonymous. Historically elusive, his figure nevertheless appears before us, irresistibly concrete and recognizable, in four songs, four terse but suggestive gospels (Isa. 42:1-4; 49:1-7; 50:4-9; 52:13-53:12).

We're still singing the same song today, for as I write this, I hear a voice on the radio describing someone from the last generation:

> he was a fascinating personality
> he stood up for the poor and oppressed
> he preached nonviolence
> but he himself was murdered.

That sounds like a pure and literal translation of:

> the Servant shares the lives of the exiles,
> for years he goes his way inconspicuously,
> unselfish, consoling, encouraging,
> firmly believing in the vision
> persistently resisting the current,
> —the rapids—
> for a short period of time he is in the news,
>   in public,
> and then everything is over, the stillness of
>   death descends:
> silence is imposed on him, for good.

The four songs of Isaiah speak of a definite human being whom a small group knew at close range and whose life took place before their eyes. After the deafening clap of his sudden disappearance, the light slowly goes on for these people: being has meaning, even being an exile. Even this situation is a mission and a calling.

The "Servant of the Lord" reveals the God of the

Covenant as the source of justice and righteousness. His life is a pure interpretation of the Living God. Such a life is the salvation of the exiles (Deut. 30:20) and their task with regard to the peoples in whose midst they must live. The Servant has demonstrated how they can turn their distress into virtue.

Their new consciousness is expressed in a "word of the Lord." The mission and promise that has been given to them is this: the Servant is themselves.

> You are my witnesses, says the Lord
>> and my servant whom I have chosen,
> that you may know and believe me
>> and understand that I am he (Isa. 43:10).

And then, in a summarizing repetition (verses 12b-13a):

> and you are my witnesses (*we-attem Edaj*),
>> says the Lord.
> (and) I am God (*we-ani El*).

These two short coordinating phrases, following the Hebrew idiom, conceal within themselves all sorts of subordinate possibilities. When you are witnesses, then (and only then) am I God. Only where people do justice is God a reality and really present in society. That was the secret of the Servant and the only possible way that a religious community can exist.

New situations can renew people, thus creating a new

access to God, but this requires many people. One person is enough, though, if that one person is a pure and concrete definition of the God of the Covenant: the unique and only loved one (*agapètos* means both beloved and the only one; Gen. 22:2), the chosen, the just—the devoted Servant whose very attributes make him son and make his life one of sonship, so he can show the way to the sonship of Israel (Exod. 4:22-23; Deut. 14:1) and the sonship of humankind.

In this way, the Exile created its own Messiah, who united the basic features of David (messianic king) and the toiling interpreter of the Torah, Moses (messianic prophet).

It would have been a great impoverishment if the New Testament had not filled itself and its Jesus figure with the Book of Isaiah, a fact that is reflected in this prophet's old Christian title of honor—of whom Jerome said that he spoke not as a prophet but as an evangelist (*non tam propheta dicendus quam evangelista*).

4 | Hebrew-Speaking Jewry
500-250 BCE
Priestly Document

From Writings to Holy Writ

The third section of the Hebrew Bible is called the Writings (*Kethuvim*). The Greek word *Hagiographa* (holy writings) is the accepted name used in the Old Church. Generally speaking, we have the post-Exilic period to thank for both the Writings and Holy Writ, which is apparent from the connection between the two terms.

Torah and the Prophets, the first two sections of the Bible, arose and grew largely through living recitation. In no respect do they have the characteristics of writings that were intentionally prepared for a reading public by a writer at his desk, although admittedly some scholars have recently maintained that they were never oral productions. Living in their own country, with permanent places and times for national meetings, everyone was within earshot of the spoken word. The dispersion (Diaspora) following the captivity (*das Exil, exilium, galut*) put an end to all that, and the normal stream bed (*Sitz im Leben*) of the Torah words and the prophetic oracles fell away.

Production and reproduction (which arise in every period of biblical development) took on a new and unique character during this first post-Exile period. The new production had the nature of writings, and the reproduction of the oral tradition now took on the character of writings, also. In short, everything became writings. The result was the Holy Writ in its present form, for both production and reproduction must pass through a final editing process (at least this is true for the Hebrew Bible). When Hebrew fell into disuse, continued growth resulted in Bibles written in contemporary languages: Aramaic and Greek.

Torah and the Prophets have a pronounced character all their own that is linked with the areas of life in which they generally arose and functioned: the covenant liturgy of the annual festal calendar. There were other areas of life that had their own specific modes of expression, however, and therefore traditions arose that cannot be categorized as either Torah or the Prophets. There was, for example, the general eastern phenomenon known as "wisdom," which was initially quite profane.

So for some time there had been an impulse toward what would become the third section of the Bible, a heterogeneous section including everything that was not Torah or the Prophets. This category was given a label capable of covering a variety of subjects: Writings. Even the label reveals something about the common feature of these heterogeneous subjects.

From Inspirations to Inspiration

Roughly speaking, the three sections of the Bible run parallel with the three main streams flowing together into the Book: Torah, Prophecy, and Wisdom. All three are of divine origin. The Scriptures apply this old eastern concept to the God of the covenant:

1. The Moses figure is a prototype of the inspired lawgiver (Exod. 19:9; 33:8-11; Deut. 5:31 or 28) as well as of the inspired prophet (Deut. 18:15-18).
2. In all the vocational stories, it is emphasized that the prophet does not speak "from his own heart" (his brain). For this reason, he is often depicted as a stutterer, uncircumcised or with tainted lips, and still almost a boy (Exod. 4:10; 6:12; Isa. 6:5-7; Jer. 1:6). Hence the formula: "The word of the Lord came to . . . " (compare 1 Sam. 3:1; Exod. 4:14-16 and 7:1-2).
3. The divine origin of Wisdom, which is later worked out in depth, is presented in advance through the Solomon figure (1 Kings 3:9-12).

Three analogous types of divine inspiration form the foundation of the growing conviction that the Book is inspired. When everything becomes Holy Writ during this period, it becomes necessary to put the new entity under one divine category. Hence it is "inspiration" in the strict sense, in which everything is applied to the Scriptures (*theopneustos;* 2 Tim. 3:16)—one common notion of inspiration for all the Scriptures.

The threefold activity of God's Spirit is thus united into one stream of divine influence directed at the Book. On closer inspection, this uniform idea turns out to be determined by characteristic prophetic inspiration. The prophet, driven by the Spirit, speaks God's word. The Scriptures, made into a book by a sacred writer who is aroused by the Spirit, contains and actually is God's word.

Because the two other forms of inspiration are thereby fitted into the idea of prophetic inspiration, prophecy is referred to technically as the "reference point" of scriptural inspiration.

Priestly Religion of the Book

This theological aside illustrates how all of life flows together in the Book, because that is just what happened during this period. The colorful national life was over and done with, but the Book remained, because everything had been put into the Book. The facts of the past, which were really quite relative (biblical history), acquired the bearing of ambiguous and even merely symbolic speech.

When people are displaced, their memory of the past is a great foothold for preserving their national identity. That is why the Book became more and more central to the temple-less and sacrifice-less liturgy of the Diaspora. Torah study had the same intention as the old sacrificial service and became a true offering in itself. In this sense, it may be said that Judaism has the features of a "religion of the book." It also explains why Jewish reproduction and final editing were so drastic and intensive.

In its new structure during this period, world Jewry looked like an international church community under the leadership of priests. After the monarchy fell away, the high priesthood became a decisive position, and the person bearing the title was the designated leader of "all Israel." Locally, the synagogue became the center of Jewish life, while the Second Temple, enriched by synagogal features, became the binding factor of a world community. Thus it is said that the priestly element became something of conclusive importance.

For centuries, serving the Torah and the altar had been preeminently priestly tasks (Deut. 33:10). But when service at the altar ceased, the new specialty of scriptural scholarship developed in priestly circles—even in Jerusalem. The metropolis could not fall behind the Diaspora, especially the Babylonian Diaspora (Neh. 8).

The Torah (*nomos* in Greek) became the heart of the synagogue and the constitutional basis of the new system. For this reason, the People of God, which had always been a theocracy, came to be typified as a "nomocracy" in Jewish form. The attitude of strict observance of the Torah, even of "one letter . . . one stroke of a letter" (Matt. 5:18) is thus called "nomism," a term that deserves an entirely different emotional value than "legalism."

The Pentateuch as Torah

A separate technical-ritualistic group tradition had developed within the priestly circles. It was a kind of sacristy legacy comparable with the rubrics, the liturgical instructions printed in "red" letters, the study and mastery of which belonged until recently to the closest preparation for service in the church. This similarity is not based only on the importance of the blood ritual.

Because the final editing of the Scriptures was mainly the work of exiled priests, their specialized legacy ended up in the Scriptures, particularly in the Pentateuch. Many a Bible reader has stumbled on this point.

The Bible was now edited with the same religious scrupulousness with which the sacrificial animal was dissected and studied in earlier times. That led to a systematization of the legacy, the introduction of broad-based and small-scale outlines, chronological and topographical scholarship, summaries and genealogies, repetitions and refrains. There's a theology in all this that includes a growing consciousness of distance with regard to the holy and devises cautious and carefully weighed formulations and illustrative descriptions. Viewed together, this scholarship produced passages that are always penetrating and often impressive.

The Pentateuch was completed around the year 400 BCE, and from that point on was unassailably canonical (and uncontested) Torah. The material already available (stories and portions of the law) was greatly expanded and reworked in the Jewish priestly spirit. The expansion consisted of collected and codified cultic-sacred prescriptions and the "Holiness Code" (Lev. 17-26), which reached deep into daily behavior and is related to the priest-prophet Ezekiel, as Deuteronomy is related to Jeremiah.

All this material is now referred to as the P document, the "Priestly Code," including especially Genesis 1, 5, 9, 17, 23; Exodus 16, 25-31, 35-40; Leviticus in its entirety; Numbers 1:1-10:10.

These P editors gave the national tradition block its current form, as far as it was reworked in the books of Exodus, Leviticus, and Numbers. They barely edited Deuteronomy, however. Instead, they did something much more radical with it: they separated Deuteronomy from the material comprising Joshua through Kings and added it to the Torah. The Pentateuch, as a totally rounded composition, is an original creation.

The Pentateuch is the literary reflection of the stability and synthesis that Jewry had reached in life. It had found a way—a literal *modus vivendi*—by which it could remain itself in the midst of the peoples among which it was dispersed. This is where the protective purity laws (Lev. 20:24-26) come in. By being recorded in the Book, the sacred secrets of past worship were put within everyone's grasp. The dedicated attention paid to them kept the intentions alive, as well as the consent to the covenant that Israel had previously expressed in its service of sacrifice.

On the other hand, this Pentateuch also became a program that established community within Jewish life, and it remained the constitution of the Jewish community through the centuries "on each stage of their journey" (Exod. 40:36b, 38b; Num. 9:15-23).

This is a journey that leads to the land, their destination. But the land is always something in the distance that both beckons and recedes: the land falls outside the bounds of the Torah, just as Moses is kept outside the bounds of the land.

Nevertheless, the land is an important element in the Creed concerning the threefold journey (Amos 2:10) and therefore plays a leading part in the national epic that is based on the Creed. The story of the conquest, however, is told in Joshua and the beginning of Judges. The P editors cut off a piece of the Creed. The Pentateuch is therefore a conscious creation, made by beheading the Creed, to keep the land out and bring Deuteronomy in.

Indeed, the Jewish program is a desert journey through "the wilderness of the peoples" (Ezek. 20:35), and that journey leads the people out of Egypt (distancing them from the world and its people) to Sinai, to the Torah. That is enough. That is your life (Deut. 30:20). That is your wisdom among the peoples (Deut. 4:6-8).

In exile or not, the reality of the land stands or falls with faithfulness to the Torah (Josh. 1).

The Chronicler

In our present canonical Bible, the D story ends with the Exile (2 Kings 25). The P account in the books of Ezra and Nehemiah then picks up the thread. They tell of the return of the exiles and the rebuilding of the Jewish community in Jerusalem around the Second Temple. The religious community in the desert of the world can once again gather around the holy Tent, from whence the Torah emanates (Isa. 2:3b).

The story of Numbers 2, a sketch of a map, is probably based on the arrangement of the pilgrim encampment around Jerusalem (which was most assuredly not left up to chance) during the Feast of the Tabernacles (*Sukkoth*). That map may be understood as a religious vision of a scattered national community: a new unity is necessary, one anchored deeper in the people than the superficial unity of an independent state.

Distinct priestly concern and interest determined the atmosphere of the books of Ezra and Nehemiah. The new orthodoxy that formed in Babylon was transplanted to Jerusalem, so the city could stand as a model for what constituted true Jewish life: purity from foreign stain (mixed marriages), stress on Sabbath rest, attention to the Torah as a Book, and a temple liturgy in which the sacrificial service is dutifully reported (copied from Samuel and Kings) but drowned out by music and song, so the program of the Second Temple can be used by the synagogue.

Typical is the way in which 1 Chronicles 15-16 reworks and expands the information from 2 Samuel 6. The added psalm (16:7-36)—an instructive collage from the psalter used to accompany a sacrifice—became the liturgical high point. This served to drown out the sacrifice, because the synagogue was forced to carry on without sacrifice. They had to learn to use the hymn that once accompanied the sacrifice as a sort of "sacrifice of desire." This "Diaspora sacrifice" was just as effective as the old sacrifice, because the singing expressed the disposition that had always made the sacrifice pleasing to God.

In the atmosphere in which this new production came to life, the old story was also revised in the two books of Chronicles. This story principally used genealogies to give a summary of all history from Adam to David, retelling the rest of the story in detail. It teems with Levites, musical instruments, and resounding hymns.

Unfavorable information about David and Solomon was passed over, and the entire story of the Northern Kingdom was omitted. Everything was told from the vantage point of temple and liturgy and from the Davidic-messianic perspective. The result is idealization, because the story was intended to serve as norm and program, no matter what happened. Sample Nehemiah 8 once again as an example of synagogue celebration, with joy because of the Torah in the midst of oppression.

Along with Ezra and Nehemiah, Chronicles forms a literary and theological whole that has come to be called "Chronistic history." The writer of these three books of the Bible is known as the "Chronicler."

This entire body of work gives a pure impression (one not influenced by other currents) of the P style and the P mentality, which makes the hand of the P editors easier to recognize in other places, especially in the Pentateuch.

Festal Scrolls and Wisdom

The Writings section contains twelve biblical books, with the three by the Chronicler taking up the rear. There are three leaders (Luke 24:44) that traditionally compete for first place: Psalms, Proverbs, Job. The middle group consists of "the five scrolls" and Daniel.

Traditionally, the Book of Esther is the preeminent festal scroll (for *Purim*)—*the* scroll, whose mere existence is responsible for the same kind of designation for all five. The order that was accepted was determined by the festal calendar: the Song of Songs (for *Pesach,* Passover), Ruth (for *Shavuoth,* Pentecost), Lamentations (on the ninth day of the summer month of Av, the commemoration of the destruction of both temples; compare with the Wailing Wall), Ecclesiastes (for Sukkoth, the Feast of Tabernacles), and Esther.

The starting point for this whole section might have been an already existing nucleus of psalms and proverbs. These texts had accompanied Israel's development since the very beginning, and the biblical books just mentioned reflect that fact.

The Book of Proverbs betrays its own past history (25:1; 30:1; 31:1). We read "the proverbs of Solomon" and "these are other proverbs of Solomon" (10:1; 25:1); hear "the words of the wise" and "these also are sayings of the wise" (22:17; 24:23). Somehow, the book took on its present size during this period, as well as its inner unity. This is especially due to the synthetical dissertation (Prov. 1-9) which, by way of prologue, opens a new view on the now collected older group of texts.

The synthesis consists in the fact that Wisdom—dealing sensibly with earthly reality—becomes saturated with respect for the Creator and for the God of the covenant. Reverently listening to reality becomes an expression of the fear of the Lord, and this is now the beginning (the main point and principle) of all wisdom. Here is where the decisive equalization of Wisdom with Torah takes place (Deut. 4:6-8; Ecclesiasticus = Sirach 24:23). This explains the flowering of Wisdom literature during this period: it glorifies faithfulness to the Torah.

The edifying story—a sort of house-and-garden lecture for the pious family—belongs here, as well. Chapters 1-6 of Daniel are examples of this; compare them with the "sapiential" climate of the Joseph story in Genesis. It is a kind of short story, also comparable with Ruth, Esther, and the narrative framework of Job during this period and, in the following period, with Tobit, Judith, and the Daniel appendixes Suzanna, Bel and the Dragon, and Daniel in the lion's den.

The case of Daniel is typical of the entire section and raises curiosity about what will happen now with the Prophets. In the Greek-Latin tradition, Daniel does indeed belong among the great prophets, but the book is nevertheless a product of writing, not preaching. The comparison with Isaiah or Jeremiah proves this at once: what is the clear reflection of a life of public appearances in Isaiah or Jeremiah is, in Daniel, the fruits of the study cell.

Apparently parts of Ezekiel also suppose a written composition, such as his visionary temple project. It's difficult to see a street preacher in Isaiah 40-66, but the oral background is unmistakable, although it seems to have existed earlier in countless conversations within a small circle. It is still living prophecy, but is adapted to the situation of exile (compare Ezek. 8:1; 14:1 and 20:1). The new form of conversation with an audience (Isa. 40:27; 49:14) began to be used with Jeremiah.

Written Prophecy

Judaism lives in the past, in the sense that its literature avails itself of the usage and style that arose during the life of the nation. Life in Canaan was many-sided, and a whole range of language and style devices developed there—a whole series of conventional patterns, each suitable to a certain situation. Many Scripture passages illustrating these patterns still survive. In the process of expanding and rewriting the Scriptures during this first Jewish period, the old-style forms continued to be used, but as a purely literary pattern. In this way, the prophetic books (the late prophets or scriptural prophets) took on their present size and form.

The oracular style, which developed through speaking and preaching, was used by writers to appeal to their reading public. The already formed collections of oracles—results of live appearances—are bound together and expanded with all kinds of written prophecy. The apocalyptic type is the most striking here.

Apocalypticism lies in the prolongation of prophecy, becoming an epigone, or imitator, almost a parasite. This leads to the tendency to compilation: new images are built up out of already available illustrative material. Some of these new images are barely imaginable, even for the most daring fantasy. We know this from the last book of the Bible, which proves conclusively that a decadent literary style can still produce an inspiring work of art and a witness worthy of belief.

The Old Scriptures have their apocalypses, as well: Isaiah 24-27, 34-35; Zechariah 12-14; and especially Daniel 7-12. These baroque texts are not something we would easily part with.

Both in style and substance, the Jewish adaptation of the prophetic heritage reflects the broader pattern. It is as if the dynamic impulse emanating from the past is made more tranquil by a sober steadiness that wants to reinterpret the seething material to fit a new situation.

The current of tradition becomes calmer, broader, clearer.

The prophets lived in a great time; their glory is that they took on the dimensions of their time. All subsequent Jewish scholarship stands on their shoulders, though it must be stated clearly that this scholarship emphasizes the Pentateuch much more than the prophets. Concentration on the prophets is more common in Christian readings of the Old Scriptures. In a few centuries of silence (500-300), they carried on their work by giving the prophetic vision a practical and livable shape, calculated on the small precept (*mitzvah*) of the ordinary life.

We do miss the explosiveness that is condensed in the prophetic oracles, but living under constant prophetic tension is simply not practicable. The Jewish texts breathe the righteousness of a life borne in faithfulness. They give us a taste of what it is like to pass on an attitude from person to person in the synagogue and the home liturgy. It's not spectacular, but make no mistake: the texts shudder and pound with a beating heart.

The creation story of Genesis 1 is just as characteristically Jewish as Daniel's synthesis of world history. The son of man acting in the name of God—a symbol of a community of faith in the Torah—holds out against all the "brutal" inhuman powers.

What appears here is the revealed secret of the Diaspora Jew. As a member of an uprooted people, and as one individual in the midst of an often hostile society, the Jew discovers the universal God of the prophets and meets God in daily life. The Jewish texts are born of this experience; they impart the knowledge of the art of living.

The Three-Phase Model

In the three periods discussed here, the Hebrew Bible took on its present shape, except for a few doubtful cases involving textual criticism. The text was now ready for the press, as it were. But the delivery of the text in handwritten and printed form was another story entirely.

In a sort of horizontal line, we see the three phases following each other in the three linking "works of history": the J story (worked into the Pentateuch), the D story (Joshua through Kings), and finally the Chronicler. All three are, stylistically and theologically, very characteristic of their periods.

A similar horizontal line can be seen in the psalter. The outer surface is determined by a series of psalms in the old "Davidic" style, mostly "I" psalms, spread over several collections including both "Yahwist" (3-41) and "Elohist" (51-65 and 68-70) texts. There are two collections of psalms with prophetic signature and allure: the collections of Korah psalms (42-49, 84-85, 87-88) and Asaph psalms (50, 73-83). Finally there is a large group of anonymous psalms (1 and 2), most of them cultic psalms from the period of the Second Temple.

A vertical buildup occurs in the three stacked layers,

but it really amounts to no more than two layers, because the old material was revised either by the prophetic school or the priestly school. The hand of D continues on from Joshua through Kings and that of P from Genesis through Numbers. Rarely, however, is a single text treated by both.

In previous explanations of this history, complicated situations that are difficult to ascertain have been reduced to a surveyable formula, yielding a picture that is faithful, manageable, and fruitful. The key to the problem is afforded by division into the three phases we have been using.

The most ancient layer of tradition, resigned to what it is, clearly defines itself. Through continued association with the Scriptures, the prophetic adaptation of the earlier period and the Jewish-priestly adaptation that followed became more and more recognizable.

It is also fascinating to see what prophetic and learned scholars have done with the old data. We begin to catch them in the act: that sort of social sensitivity is truly prophetic; this and that theology (about "the cloud of glory," for instance) is priestly, through and through. In the meantime, the notion is growing that the texts are open to being filled with our own lives.

The Three Books of the Covenant

The old book of the covenant (Exod. 20:22-23:33) shows an example of these two types of editing on a somewhat smaller scale. The text was reworked by P in the "Holiness Code" (Lev. 17-26) and by D in the Codex of Deuteronomy (12-28).

All three books of law combine two types of laws: short apodictic formulas in the second-person singular (you shall or you shall not) and third-person singular (he who does this or that must be punished in this or that way). These short laws lay scattered, in groups and sometimes individually, among casuistic formulas (if it should happen that, then . . . then . . . ; if however it should happen that, then . . .).

All three books of law exhibit an identical phenomenon. A motive is added to the formulation of the law in which the second-person singular and plural (unfortunately indistinguishable in English) are regularly alternated, a rhetorical device very typical of Deuteronomy.

A third signal that indicates various versions of the same old data lies in the construction of the three books of law.

1. All three begin with a sort of sanctuary or altar law (Exod. 20:24-26). Deuteronomy 12 contains the famous law of the single altar, anchored in the Sinai story by Leviticus 17:1-9.
2. Then come all sorts of social laws alternating with laws having to do with governing the sacred and the taboo.
3. After these come alternating apodictic and casuistic formulas.

4. Finally, all three are rounded off with a blessing
   and a curse (Exod. 23:20-33; Lev. 26; Deut.
   27-28).

Leviticus 19 does credit to its name, "the little Torah,"
by containing all these elements.

Now comes the more detailed work. The casuistic
elements of Deuteronomy 15:12-18 and 19:4-7 are a
reworking of those in Exodus 21:1-11 and 21:12-14. A
larger section is reworked in Deuteronomy 20-25. There
we find a whole section of "family legislation" that is
almost completely missing in Exodus or, rather, has
fallen away.

Exodus 22:16-17 (or 15-16), the end of a larger group
of casuistic laws, is the only text that touches on family
relationships, probably the impulse for a whole series
that could have been reconstructed from Deuteronomy
20-25. It is obvious that Deuteronomy rendered part of
the covenant Book of Exodus superfluous, and the part
was consequently lost. This covenant book is then a
"torso": it has not survived in its entirety.

We are interested here in three versions of a covenantal
document that was used in the liturgy and, by being so
used, underwent a growth process: one version kept
replacing the previous one. The Deuteronomy document replaced that of Exodus, as did that of Leviticus.
We see D and P at work, each in his own milieu.

The broad outlines of D and P run parallel to each
other. Both reworked the old block of traditional texts

without getting in each other's way, because they each had their own time and place. P's final editing occurred later than that of D and in D's wake. Deuteronomy bridges the gap between prophet (D) and priest (P) by channeling the prophetic torrent and forcing it into a priestly stream bed. The torrent is redirected to the small duties (*mitzvah*) of everyday life (Buber).

Approached somewhat differently, this important biblical information can be described in this way. The relationship between Jeremiah, the priest from Anatot, and the priest-prophet Ezekiel has a parallel in the literary fact that the prophetic spirit of the covenantal document in Deuteronomy seems to be the inspiration for the priestly covenantal document in Leviticus. This is thus an expression (on a smaller scale) of the parallel relationship between D and P. Interpreted as an equation (for those who are interested), it looks like this: D : P = Jer. : Ezek. = Deut. : Lev. = Deut. 12-28 : Lev. 17-26.

The covenantal Book of Exodus fell into disuse; the Deuteronomy covenantal book took over its function. But there was still a large piece (although just a torso) that was recovered when the final editors, for whom each document was important, completed the Scriptures. Wasn't the idea to salvage as much of the past as possible?

This rather complicated example gives us a look at a typical phenomenon: the careful recording of what is still left and the search for fragments among the debris. An excellent example of this is the decalogue recorded in Exodus 20 and Exodus 34, and there are other examples of several complete or incomplete versions of the same data that have survived. Figuring all this out is no superfluous luxury, because each version takes up the task with the Scripture in its present form, within its new context.

The vast construction of the Sinai story is partly determined by this phenomenon. The final editors saw the chance to link up all the available documents—the result of diligent detective work—to the great meeting of Moses with the Lord on the summit of the holy mountain of revelation:

1. The linking text for the "ethical" decalogue is Exodus 20:1 and 18, once again underscored by Exodus 24:12 and 31:18;
2. The linking text for the old book of the covenant is Exodus 20:21 or 18, reinforced by the small addition of "rights" (ordinances or regulations) in Exodus 24:3;
3. The design of the tabernacle (Exod. 25-31); linking text Exodus 24:18;
4. The "cultic" decalogue (Exod. 34:17-26 = 23:10-19) with its well-known linking text Exodus 34:1-5 and 27-28 (who is writing this, the Lord or Moses?).

All the documents, whatever their condition, were worked into the story, although the earlier scholars turned their most beloved document into the actual subject of the conversation between the Lord and Moses.

Besides this, it was the priestly tradition to feature the texts that interested them most (the holy tent with the cloud and the glory of God)—compare Exodus 24:12-18 with Exodus 40:34-38.

5 | Greek-Speaking Jewry
After 250 BCE
The Septuagint

The Hebrew Bible was now completed, to the extent that the Torah and the Prophets were canonical, but the group of writings remained elastic until its canonization process was sealed at the end of the first century CE. That was a matter that remained within the circle of Judaism, for the young church, following the Hellenistic Diaspora, used the translation of "the Seventy," the Septuagint (often referred to by the roman numeral "LXX"), whose origin will be discussed here.

Translation or New Original Text?

The theory of scriptural inspiration, which was jealously guarded by dogmatic theologians who only reluctantly entrusted it to exegetes, played a trick on us. One of the claims of this theory is that only the original text is inspired; translations of the original are not. How far this theoretical blindness can lead may be seen in the following example.

We know by chance from a few historic witnesses that Matthew first wrote a gospel in Hebrew (i.e., Aramaic; Acts 21:40 and 22:2). None of this text has survived. An illustrious theologian, champion of orthodoxy, teaches us in his textbook on inspiration that the Hebrew gospel was beyond all doubt an inspired text. But, he continues, that claim cannot be made for our gospel of Matthew, because that is a translation. The inspiration for this translation is therefore not a point of doctrine; it's nothing but what was once called "pious opinion," leaving us with a good example of "the heresy of orthodoxy."

It must be emphatically stated that after the Hebrew Bible was in place, the process of scriptural expansion and revision continued uninterrupted. New books were born, and a new translation was made of the existing books (i.e., the Hebrew Bible) which was, in fact, a new version, a new reading of the scriptural legacy, one created in a more developed religious climate and grounded in very different soil: the Greek language.

This is an almost inconceivable revolution, however much in line with the worldwide tendency of the prophetic vision. But it must have given rise to the feeling that Israel's individuality—so costly and so jealously guarded—was hanging in the balance now that it had been made accessible to the other peoples of the world.

Instead of the five cities of Egypt using the language of Canaan as their mother tongue (Isa. 19:18 has even fewer linguistic pretensions than Gen. 11:1 and should be understood in the sense of Ps. 87:4, in which Rahab stands for Egypt), the sons of Israel in the Diaspora helped themselves to the unclean language of the heathens (Josh. 22:19; 1 Sam. 26:19; Ps. 137:4).

These sorts of things cannot be invented or deliberately organized. They just happen, and you can't prevent them from happening or try to undo them. A Jerusalem Jew would have to find out how to return to a life of purity under these circumstances and how to reconcile the situation with his or her familiar way of thinking about the faith.

Few were successful in pulling this off. Wherever the new situation was most intense, it was a matter of bend or break, or a question of dying out with an irrevocably lost history. Jerusalem could not object to the Diaspora; the most it could do was to hold it in contempt, beginning with Galilee (John 7:41, 49, 52). In the end, the Diaspora would become the center of events, the principal bearer of the religious tradition.

The Septuagint is the literary reflection of the Diaspora. In retrospect, this turned out to be a prelude and transition to a new fact that is even more compelling and disconcerting, one connected with the coming Second Destruction. The big breakthrough that took place in the Diaspora on the occasion of the First Destruction had to be recovered in all its purity, if the people of Israel

wanted to be equal to the unprecedented new situation
that established itself at the time of the Second Destruction, when the peoples of the world just walked right
into the community of faith and pitched their tents as if
it were their own territory (Gen. 9:27).

But early in this period that hadn't happened yet. No
one suspected how important it would be for the people
to learn to spell Ky-ri-e e-le-ison beside the familiar
Adonai *chonnénu.* To approach the Septuagint, one must
look at things on a broad scale, definitely not in an
academic way. The Septuagint is as good an original text
as our Greek Matthew.

The Targum Phenomenon

During this period, Hebrew was the language of the
synagogue liturgy and the scholars, a situation comparable with that of Latin since the early Middle Ages, with
its Church Latin and the Latin of the Clerks. When the
Torah was read aloud, the practice gradually grew of
providing an extemporaneous (oral) translation of each
verse in the vernacular. This was also done, usually after
every three verses, with the closing reading (the
haphtarah) from the Prophets (Luke 4:17; Acts 13:15,
27; 15:21). In time, these improvised translations took
on a definite form. They became a standard translation
that was later made available in written form, although
it had to be recited from memory, in order to differen-
tiate it from the genuine Scriptures.

These translations were made in Aramaic, the linguistic vehicle of the semitic East. The ones that still survive are called Targums, translations. This term is visibly related to the Arabic word *dragoman* or *drogman,* a technical term for an interpreter at an embassy or consulate, especially in the eastern and Turkish world.

Three complete Targums of the Pentateuch have survived: a Babylonian (Onkelos) and two Palestinian (Pseudo-Jonathan and, discovered in 1956, Neofiti). They are at their most fascinating where they depart from the Hebrew text. Sometimes this deviation is so extreme that they take on the character of a midrash. Indeed, early versions of many later midrashim can be recognized in the Targums, so they are not only textual witnesses (they reach much further into the past than the Hebrew Bible manuscripts), but they grant a look into the exegesis of the time.

In the Hellenistic Diaspora, especially in Egypt (Alexandria), Greek was read in the places where Aramaic was read in the East. A verbal Greek translation was used, sometimes harking back to the Aramaic tradition of translation, sometimes not, because in the long run, it was difficult to go on without Palestinian help.

It is obvious that in some synagogues no one could read the Hebrew letters any more, for there are manuscripts in which the Hebrew was transliterated in Greek letters. The Hexapla of Origen (d. 254), containing six versions of the biblical text in six columns, gave this transliteration in the second column. There are few fragments of this manuscript remaining, but they are instructive about how Hebrew was pronounced at that time, because Greek included vowels as well as consonants, unlike Hebrew. In short, a Greek Targum must have been created.

The Greek Targum

The Septuagint had a very good reputation in Diaspora circles. Its inspired authority was substantiated by the famous story (the letter of Aristeas) of the 72 scholars from Jerusalem (6 from each tribe) who were sent to the peninsula of Pharos in Alexandria and locked up in 72 huts. At the end of 72 days, each scholar had translated the entire Bible into Greek; all the translations were completely identical.

This story was taken literally for a very long time, which must have contributed to the fact that only in the last century did the origin of the Septuagint become an open question. It was the contour of the Septuagint itself—very unevenly translated from book to book—that led to the conclusion that the principal matrix of the Septuagint must have been a Greek Targum.

Without ruling out the possibility that some central authority exercised a hand in the final developmental phase of the Septuagint, the text can safely be regarded as a complete, preserved Greek Targum.

The inspiration of a book is derivative, since inspiration is a charisma of human beings. The whole question boils down to how seriously you take the religious community that brought forth the book and invested its very best in it.

The Septuagint is more than a translation; it is a new faith witness. Its inspiration is more than merely offering a pure reproduction of the original Hebrew text. It is completely inspired, even in those places—especially in those places—where it goes its own way.

Its Targum character underscores its religious value, because it is this particular quality that carries with it the voice of a widespread religious community through many generations.

Seven New Books

In addition to all this spontaneous and creative reproduction, this period also produced seven new books. Some of them originated in Greek (Wisdom and 2 Maccabees), and for that reason had no chance of ever becoming Holy Scripture within Palestinian circles. Most were written in Hebrew or Aramaic. Jerome knew 1 Maccabees in its Hebrew version. The Hebrew version of Sirach was popular among Jews until the Middle Ages. We owe our knowledge of this to the fact that around 1900, three-quarters of the Hebrew book was recovered. But apparently these Hebrew books were born too late to have a chance at inclusion in the Hebrew (or Palestinian) canon.

In their Greek translation, however, they captured a permanent place in Hellenistic synagogues, so they did end up in the Greek (or Alexandrian) canon and thus in the Septuagint. The seven books are 1 and 2 Maccabees, the Wisdom of Solomon, the Wisdom of Sirach (Ecclesiasticus), Judith, Tobit, and Baruch, plus a few additions to Esther and Daniel.

This innocent little list makes one ask, "Is this what they made such a fuss over for so many centuries? What difference does it make?" Well, it makes a lot of difference in a theory of belief where each word is the word of God. One of the gruesome consequences of this belief deserves a closer look. It was always an absurdity of Catholic theology after the Council of Trent that the scriptural character of these books (considered doubtful in the ancient church) became an explicit and important point of doctrine. Oddly, "scriptural authority" was attached to the vast remainder of the Septuagint, even though that had always been recognized as Scripture by the ancient church, only insofar as these books were pure reflections of the Hebrew original.

Within the business of theology during the last centuries, this was not something that stayed within the realm of theory. The Septuagint was not read for its own sake. Whatever deviated from the Hebrew in the Septuagint did not come under attention. People were blind to the fact that each Greek passage is a separate creation, both literarily and theologically, and that tasting each one for its own character and expressiveness is definitely a worthwhile activity.

The Bible of the Eastern Church

This is another aspect in which the schism between East and West, in addition to being rather unnecessary, proved to be fatal. The Septuagint, first Bible of the apostolic Primitive Church, was and remained for centuries the Bible of the East and the Greek Fathers. The medieval Latin church had little notion of this, since for it the church was the Western church. A small and extreme example here might serve as a beacon at sea for our Roman church situation, as for a stranded ship.

During the years 1514-1517, the Alcala Bible, the first Polyglot (multilanguage) Bible was printed. The folio pages are divided into three columns. In the preface we read:

> We have placed the Latin translation of Jerome in the middle column, and in the side columns "the Hebrew truth" and "the Seventy"; the Synagogue on the one side, as it were, and the Eastern Church on the other; thus on each side a murderer (*latro*), and so in the middle Jesus (John 19:18), that is, the Roman or Latin Church.

To see the Septuagint in the broadest light, the church must be seen in the broadest light. The church, with the East first, is more than a colony of Latium. Rather, the relationship is just the other way around—at least in Greek eyes.

"Hebrew Truth"

Reformed Protestant tradition is much more burdened with leaden biblical theories than Catholic tradition. This burden has given rise to the deep-seated modern tendency to exaggerate "the Hebrew truth." To deal with this, however, we first need some background.

Humanism around the time of the Renaissance was in love with the original biblical languages. The protest against Rome found literary expression in the rejection of the Latin Vulgate, which had been declared a reliable expression of belief by the Council of Trent. That is the substance of the so-called authenticity of the Vulgate.

The actual consequence of this rejection is that our Protestant brothers went on to make marvelous translations straight from the original text, while the Counter-Reformation had to make do with translations from Latin. It wasn't until this century that Catholic translations were made from the original text.

In the Netherlands, for example, the first translation from the original text was published by the Peter Canisius Society and included the Gospels and Acts (1906), the entire New Testament (1929), and the entire Old Testament (around 1940). Finally, the Canisius Society became the more ecumenical Catholic Biblical St.

Willibrord Foundation, which produced an entirely new translation (1961-1972).

With this background, it's a bit easier to understand how the adventures in the growth of the Scriptures developed into one of the issues over which confessional groups waged trench warfare against one another for centuries.

An overrating of "the Hebrew truth" (the expression *veritas hebraica* is constantly on the lips of the polemicizing Jerome) goes hand in hand with distrust of the Seven (the contribution of the Greek Bible). There's an exchange of letters on this point between Augustine, who was accustomed to the old Latin translation of the Septuagint, and Jerome, who champions his new Latin translation from Hebrew.

Jerome (d. 420)

The unequal sizes of the Hebrew and Greek Bibles has been a problem for as long as the Bible has existed. The church of the second to fifth centuries was not equipped to find a theoretical solution. East and West came to the practical conclusion that the Seven do belong in the canon, since they had been read in the church as far back as anyone could remember and everyone believed the Bible of the apostles could not be faulty.

That the Hebrew Bible did not contain all this material only dawned on people during disputes with Judaism. This was a painful and even alarming discovery, because everything had begun in Palestine. With the obstinate partiality of the Hebrew specialist, Jerome issued a few strong statements that did not disturb the unanimity that had been reached but did lend a scrap of credibility to people who wanted to go against the grain. There's someone like that in every century, but it wasn't until the dispute with the Reformation that Jerome again became a state witness.

Jerome was a believer and a devoted son of the church who treated the Seven the same way he treated the rest of the Scriptures. He even translated Tobit and Judith, but he did it hastily and clandestinely, because doing so defied "the pharisaic eyebrow" of his Jewish teachers. However, whenever his opponents played the Septuagint against his translation, the scholar in him rose up and called the Seven mere apocrypha.

Trent (1546)

The Fathers of the Council of Trent all agreed that the thickest Bible was the best. From February to May, 1546, they disputed over whether there was any difference in degree or value among the parts of that thick Bible. Although there was general agreement that there was a difference, that difference could not be formulated into a statement.

Finally, the abbot general of an order (not a bishop!) saved the situation by saying, "When Jerome and Augustine do not agree, the church should not come between them." It was therefore decided to pass the question on intact to posterity, as it had been received from the forefathers.

Indeed, from ancient times to today, not two but three kinds of books have been identified:

1. books that have been recognized at all times and by everyone (*homologoumena*);
2. books that for shorter or longer periods, and in a few places, were doubted, not read, or rejected (*antilegomena*);
3. books that have been and continue to be unanimously regarded as not genuine (pseudo-, apocryphal).

During the late Middle Ages, the terms *protocanonical* and *deuterocanonical* were invented to describe the first two groups.

Deuterocanonical or Apocryphal

In the controversy that has continued since the Reformation, the Seven became a traditional point of dispute. Currently we only know the hardened points of view, but initially, everything was much more flexible and subject to a great deal of discussion. Early Protestant versions of the Bible commonly contained warnings for those who would read the apocryphal books.

Eventually the apocrypha were omitted altogether

from the Bibles intended for ordinary use in Reformed homes. This set the trend, except for the Lutherans, who stayed with their Luther Bible.

Although in the beginning there was still a bit of theoretical and practical openness on both sides, today people seem to agree that the intertestamental literature (to which the Seven belong) is of interest to everyone. This whole antiquated problem draws attention to the "chance factor" in the birth of the Scriptures: *Some books just make it into the canon; others don't.*

The New Testament now has the same size everywhere. Nevertheless, in the formation of the New Testament canon, chance plays an even clearer role. On entirely different grounds than those concerning the Old Testament, and with just as little basis in one common ground, a few books of the New Testament (again seven) were considered dubious. Those held to be deuterocanonical were Hebrews and the Apocalypse, James and Jude, 2 and 3 John, and 2 Peter.

Even though the church finally adhered to the larger canon, a distinction arose between the books that were and were not useful in conversations with Judaism. This distinction led to this formula: there are books that can be used to defend the *faith;* there are also books which the church reads in order to instill good *morals* and for the formation of young people. That sounds reasonable, because the disputed group belongs to the strongly moralizing third section of the Bible (sometimes called the "Writings"). For a long time, this group was referred to as ecclesiastical, a term that lives on in the Vulgate, where it became the name of the preeminently ecclesiastical book Sirach (called *Ecclesiasticus* in Latin).

It wasn't until the Middle Ages that the translation of Jerome found general acceptance. Whatever the church fathers had not translated was then supplemented with the translation that had gradually grown out of the Septuagint during the second century. The *Editio Vulgata* is therefore medieval, as far as the name and the subject (its propagation) are concerned.

Circulation

Concerning these controversies, only one attitude leads to a solution with any prospects—considering the Septuagint as a full-fledged Scripture with its own contribution to the faith. It faces the fact that, just as Hebrew-speaking Jewry had done, so Greek-speaking Jewry also formed a community that became a worthy bearer of the religious tradition. This community is absolutely indispensable, because it is the link that binds the Hebrew congregation with the first Christian congregation, from which the Greek New Testament was born.

One and the same inspiration maintains the people of God through the centuries, no matter how the sociological structures in which the congregation of God lives change. Depending on the historical situation, this people takes on a tangible form, by which it becomes incarnate in its particular situation and finds a particular embodiment.

As this sketch makes clear, the scriptural process takes root in the movement of faith, with all its various possibilities of expression. The inspiration that gives rise to books stands or falls with the inspiration of the human group in which the books come to life.

The irreplaceable linking function of Diaspora Jewry expresses itself on a literary level through the linking function of the Septuagint—situated as it is between the Hebrew Bible and the Greek New Testament. Without the Septuagint, there can be no New Testament.

The Scriptural Whole: Nucleus and System of Rings

The Scriptures, in the view being proposed here, are one coherent literary-historical and theological phenomenon, much more inclusive than we are accustomed to thinking because we are accustomed to use many kinds of separate editions for large parts of the whole.

The total phenomenon is given birth to by the Hebrew Bible, which is its center, its matrix, and its rootstock. A broad wreath has formed around this center, one made up of documents that increasingly take on a midrashlike character and join together in one Greek Bible, such as those handed down in the fourth and fifth centuries with their famous uncial or majuscule handwriting:

1. the translation of the Hebrew Bible;
2. the intertestamentary writings;
3. and with the New Testament as the closing piece.

This Greek group belongs to the innermost system of rings formed around the Hebrew Bible, which is the magnetic nucleus. This great whole forms the one complete book of faith documentation that has been passed down to us. The formulated parts penetrate one another so that even the smallest part gets its full authority only from the whole.

The Targums and the midrashim are also entrances to the scriptural data. They belong to the phenomenon, as well, and should be involved in exegesis. Although laid down during the postbiblical period, they still have their roots in the centuries before our era (it appears from the Septuagint that their fruitful fields lie around the Second Temple).

Then there are the biblical "aftereffects"—the later reworkings that are also entrances to scriptural data and are primary documents in addition to the Vulgate and the other old translations, the exegesis of the Fathers, the liturgies of the East and the West, and even the King James Version. Four great and classic Polyglot Bibles prove that this insight is not new: Alcala (1517), Antwerp (1572), Paris (1645), and, the last and the greatest, London (1657).

Part 3 | **THE STUDY HOUSE OF THE WORD**

6 | An "Open House" for Biblical Studies

The New Testament from the Bottom Up

When you set off on the path of the Old Scriptures, you pass through the back gate (and only the Old Scriptures have the key) into New Testament territory. Taking that path, you can be astounded, find it hard to believe your eyes. You've been through the New Testament often enough, but you always entered by the great front gate that centuries of theology, art, and piety have erected on the unshakable foundations of four early ecumenical councils.

But now you are just walking, so to speak, directly into the synagogue and into the household of Nazareth. You recall everything you've read in the New Testament, including the final drama of the life of Jesus in Jerusalem. You begin to feel that after years and years of taking the construction of those events for granted you have to get something off your chest. You want to write to the ministers, priests, and teachers of your childhood to ask:

"What was done to Jesus? What we were taught in Catechism and Sunday School ought to have been correct. How were we allowed to miss this?"

In retrospect, you remember that what we were told back then was what *theology* had to tell us. Theology in the twenties and thirties wasn't, to be sure, all bad. It gave you the opportunity to delve deep into the Scriptures and the Fathers. You got to know Thomas Aquinas, "the Angelic Doctor," quite well. But what most really got was an overview of popular *manual theology*. Certainly it was a sturdy stockade, behind whose secure boundaries every doctrine had its place and theological "note" assigned to tell you its degree of "certainty."

Theology then had the appearance of a continuous dispute, with heretics and various shades of dangers. Argument is a good thing, but disputes such as those that theology tended to carry on risked working so much with intellectual concepts that in the end they gave the impression that what theology was about was "proving" that a given body of opinion was "right."

Reality, at least the reality of religious faith, however, is much deeper and broader than doctrines that can be "proved." Ultimately, religious reality is reached only through the gate of narrative, myth, and symbol. Conceptualist theology can only go part way toward mediating contact with such reality.

Taking its origins in the study of the history of religions and "first-order" religious language, the term "myth," in the past fifty years, has taken on a positive meaning in biblical studies. Meanwhile, even if only sporadically at first, the term *midrash* made an appearance. Both terms in fact allude to the power of "narrative" and "story" as indispensable means by which religious truth and value are transmitted. Thus we find ourselves confronted by today's so-called "narrative" or "story" theologies.

The Bible *is* narrative. Dogmatic formulae, on the other hand, are built from carefully crafted, interlocking sets of ideas whose apparent clarity and logic can be deceptive. It is easy to forget that their origins are concrete, not abstract. They arise in long-gone mindsets and metaphors that were astoundingly fresh before they became hardened into concepts distilled from complicated, often nearly forgotten events in ages long past.

This is how you find yourself reflecting on what really counts in what I want to call "the Nazareth study house." What you learn in that house can have such a positive effect that you will feel no need to delete a jot or tittle from the tradition you grew up in. What you will experience in the Nazareth study house is that the tradition itself has been growing considerably.

Insight into the perpetual growth of tradition, however, leads you to look at what you received in a different way. Tradition is then seen in a much fuller content, that of the re-presentational expressiveness of *midrash,* a beloved *midrash* with basilicas, abbeys, cathedrals, and Gregorian chant. We can keep on using all the old traditions, singing the old tunes, as long as we sing them well and don't wield them like axes in a one-dimensional, bad-tempered reaction to the contemporary world.

In short, our tradition's history is good as long as it continues to be a story of faith, a theological story in which the *theo*logy is drawn from the Old Scriptures, the only place where we can find out what kind of *god* Jesus addresses as Abba. Because whenever the New Testament calls Jesus "the Son of God," it means the Son of *that* God.

"Son of God": A Christmas or an Easter Title

The title "Son of God" is particularly useful because it gives us an entrée to the metaphor with which we started—the back and the front gates.

Seen from the Old Scriptures, this title tells us that Jesus spent his life pursuing the path of Justice and Righteousness. That's why he can be called the "son" of the God of the Covenant, whose Name is defined— functionally or operationally—in the entire body of Scripture by the mission to achieve justice in human and human-divine relationships.

This Jesus does his utmost to make this God a tangible reality in our human world—placing God before us as the horizon of all our life and work. Whenever we do the same, we are, together with Jesus, sons and daughters of the same God, and we may call him Father, as Jesus does.

The title "Son of God" is, in the first place, an existential and social one, moveable and dynamic. Eventually it is used as a retrospective legitimization of the completed lifework of Jesus. It is at one level an Easter title (Ps. 2:7 in Acts 13:33), but at its roots it is an anticipatory (proleptic) Baptismal title (Mt. 3:17) or a Tabor title (Mt. 17:5).

This Jesus, according to the New Scriptures, has been made and declared the Son, Lord, and Messiah (Acts 2:36; Rom. 1:4; Phil. 2:9-11)—his "glorification" marked by the proclamation implicit in the title. Moreover, his name entails a platform. In Jesus the Son of God, according to New Testament theology, the meaning and mission of humankind on earth is revealed.

This approach, however, which is quite visible in the New Testament, can be drowned out by a second approach to Jesus that occurs in a certain kind of later, often post-biblical development. The title increasingly was frozen in essentialist, sacred, and static categories. It was linked speculatively to supposedly eternal relationships which precede Jesus' life and work on earth. In such images, the Son was portrayed as having existed with God throughout eternity (pre-existence). Thus the Easter title became a Christmas title that was understood principally as having something to tell us about the divine personhood of Jesus (see Ps. 2:7 taken over into Heb. 1:5 and 5:5; parallel with Ps. 110:4 taken over into Heb. 5:6; 7:17 and 21).

In that adoption Jesus is portrayed as high-born, beyond the state of us ordinary humans. By the grace of Baptism we become his adopted children, according to the image of *this* pre-existent Son. As tradition develops, this will result in the theological formula "we are by grace what the Son is by nature." The older approach can still be heard in this statement, however, because in its negative formulation, we are denied this kind of filial relationship to God if we do not make it real through acts of justice and righteousness.

These two approaches do not exclude each other. Both can be used correctly, in fact, as *supplements* to one another and when kept in tension. But what *does* the average believer think when he or she hears mention of "the Son of God"? Because of a one-sided emphasis, the second, the Christmas, approach has gone on to lead a life of its own. Thus, instead of being a helpful complementary or supplementary theological *midrash,* it has taken on a factual, historical character that barely reminds us of the mission of Jesus in this world. It evokes an article of faith by means of which Christians identify themselves over against other religious traditions and bodies.

Oikonomia and *Theologia*

The Eastern Church has done a great deal of work on the distinction between "economy" and theology. *Oikonomia,* still recognizable in the technical term "the economy of salvation" (the "charity" or the "system" of salvation), alludes to information from history. This is the only valid entrance to theology, because only by exploring our earthly reality—which we do see—can we make a meaningful "working sketch" of the divine world—which we glimpse only darkly and indirectly—in something like the way scientific instruments explore and examine their objects, interpreting the information received in code, speaking meaningfully of things known only indirectly.

This way of processing data produces reliable working hypotheses and formulae, graphic presentations—graphics representing realities that we have not seen, but which offer a foothold for the religious insight that our symbols, stories, and myths reflect reality—if you can "read" or "decode" them.

Long ago, however, certain theological formulae won the day. And they have been repeated unchanged for fifteen centuries: definitive, massive, opaque, more scholarship than proclamation, runaway concepts that can only be harnessed by confronting them with the narratives, symbols, and myths of the Old Scriptures.

Such formulae can enfeeble our confession of faith when they are presented as pronouncements about Jesus in ways that no longer excite the imagination, stir the heart, or open the door of faith that leads to the future. *We only understand the story of Jesus correctly when we realize that it is our story, too.* And that should apply all the more to the conceptual formulae which we use to help us touch the core of the story of Jesus.

But lest I be taken as hostile to every use of such formulae, recall the beautiful, powerful experience of hearing the cultic language of the Latin creed—*Deum de Deo, lumen de lumine, Deum verum de Deo vero* ("God from God, light from light, true God from true God").

Sung untranslated in the context of the Mass—within the entirety of our story of faith (which is more than a body of conceptually rendered "truths")—these words take on the suggestive surplus of meaning one finds in *midrash*. No need to throw out babies with bath water!

A Theological Midrash on Humanity

Thanks to the "interpersonal" movement that is the essence of their existence, Abba/Father, Son, and Spirit have for centuries led a completely happy life. Their desire is to let others participate in their happiness by creating them in their own image. And so it was that humanity came into being. By attentively following the work of their hands, the three divine persons see—age in and age out—how people are born and die, how they thirst after each other's blood and treasure, and thus are doomed in droves. That's not a situation to be dealt with theoretically from Olympian distance. Looked at scripturally, it requires that something practical be done. Thus our *midrash:*

> After their first deliberation, "Let us make Adam," comes the second decision: "Let us bring about human deliverance." But then: "Whom shall we send? And who shall go for us?" Not a simple problem.
>
> Accompanied by Justice, Truth hurries to the throne of God; soon Mercy arrives, quite

out of breath and accompanied by Peace. It becomes a full judicial procedure. Truth insists that Justice must run its course. Mercy pleads that God is bound to decide what makes for Peace in the lives of human beings.

The Father is stuck in the middle and turns the case over to his Son, who is Wisdom personified. Both parties agree with Wisdom's finding—an innocent party will volunteer to take on the deserved punishment. And so it is written: "Steadfast love and faithfulness will meet; Righteousness and peace will kiss each other" (Ps. 85:10).

Now to find an innocent party who has so much love that he will sacrifice himself for human beings. Consultation follows with the nine angelic choirs. A search over the face of the earth and even a visit to the bosom of Abraham are fruitless. Time passes. No solution is in sight. What happens then is something that no one could have expected or even imagined. The Son reports to the Father: "Here am I. Send Me" (Is. 6:8; Heb. 10:7, citing Ps. 40:7-9).

And the Father sends him, and he is realized by the Spirit in the virgin's womb, and the Son shows the people how to live together (Jn. 15:12-13). So it happens that "since Abel" people have been found who are identifiable as an "image" of the Trinitarian God (see "We"

and "Us" in Gen. 1:26 and Is. 6:8; compare
Gen. 18:2).

This half-Jewish, half-Patristic midrash—admittedly
suffused with patriarchal and sacrificial imagery—is
composed of information about the way of our world
(*oikonomia,* whence "economy"). The narrative structure places it in the divine world (as theo-logia, talk
about God's ways). In the process, to the eyes of faith,
our world has become transparent.

Seen through the theological magnifying glass of the
first ecumenical councils, the Son of God is the eternal
Word, substantially identical with the Father. His whole
"personhood" consists in being "spoken" by the Father
so that he, with the pure and faultless "imprint" of God
on him (Heb. 1:3), is the complete revelation of God's
name, as "Word," God's heart on God's tongue (Jn.
1:18).

This theological *midrash* is an explanation that is built
on historic material. The Jewish person Jesus of Nazareth
is principally an interpretation of the God of the Covenant. As such, he reveals the most intimate and sensitive
places in God's heart, because of God's concern to take
the oppressed (Ex. 3) to Godself, the mainspring and life
of divine life (Jn. 4:34). To do the righteous work of
Abba—that's what Jesus lives for, that is his meat and
drink. That is why this summary applies to the whole
life of Jesus—this man is truly just (Lk. 23:47), or to put
it another way, truly the Son of God (Mk. 15:39).

The mission of justice and righteousness is the first

and last word of the Scriptures and must be first in the very core of living, creative religious tradition. Otherwise tradition as dead weight will keep us from our work.

The Horror of Devastation

The concept of "god" in the Old Scriptures rests on a thorough secularization of preunderstandings general in a highly sacralized society of the ancient near East. No matter how problematic a burden it is in the contemporary world, "secularization" in this instance is positive. It sees to it that "god" really has meaning again.

Biblically speaking, God and humanity are discovered and defined together. Indeed they are in continual exchange, but there is still a certain order: from the authentically human to the authentically divine and, only "then," the other way around. Through the imitation of God the human individual reaches full development, but he has to make sure that he has taken the "good" god as an example.

The word "God," then, has human content, and divinity is given a name that describes how people should live together. The Jesus story continues this line of thought. Jesus is primarily a revelation of the ancient God of the Covenant, and the answer to our question of who Jesus really is can only come from this God, and not from a universal idea of "god." The narratives in *these* Scriptures mediate to us ever-growing knowledge of the identity of *this* God.

But even this God does not escape the danger of becoming a common and facile idea. For the pious and the impious, in ecclesiastical, liturgical, and even biblical language, "God" runs the risk of ending up in a too sacred realm, as if Godself can be envisaged apart from human efforts to live justly, mercifully, and lovingly with one another in the everyday world.

Since the everyday world is both our own and God's home, secularization should not be an alarming process. Furthermore, insight into that reality forces us to ask why we're often so busy involving ourselves in "churchy" matters. Since I have more than once found myself in arguments with traditionalists, who almost seem to want to put a knife to my throat when they ask, "Do you still believe in the divinity of Christ?", I understand the repugnance that the kind of thing I've been saying evokes. But I can only say, "It's that exalted 'god' of yours that worries me. I don't want to jeopardize Jesus by associating him with it, either. We both need to be liberated by the biblical God of justice."

In the Bible you cannot find a separate "god of philosophers" apart from "the God of Abraham." But that dictum pushes you into a corner with a god who is known only through dealings with humanity, an extremely ambiguous and dangerous realm. But with this Jesus we know where we are, and we know what God we're talking about. For the New Testament has Jesus say, "The one who sees me has seen the Father"; and, "I am come to make known the Name of my Father among human beings." That's why Jesus is the Way.

Jesus is the point of departure because he is a known and an unambiguous factor. He has led an earthly life, and no one can get around that. He is held up as a sign (Lk. 2:34-35). We have a detailed story about him that witnesses its own and his authenticity.

So, the unknown is defined by the known, not the other way around. This Jesus we know shows the nature of the one we so frequently misunderstand. For the New Testament, Jesus is the concrete "definition" *of God.*

The saying, "Jesus is God," however, turns this around and impresses itself on us as a "definition" *of Jesus.* The shift is subtle and dangerous, defining what we know by what is intrinsically mysterious, known only obliquely through myth, symbol, and narrative. Declaring Jesus to be a divine creature constitutes a danger that we will lose Jesus if we don't know everything important about God.

This is a careless use of language that is best avoided. It drives Jesus into an unpredictable sacred corner. The saying that Jesus is God, *as we Christians normally hear that affirmation,* gives short shrift to the human dimension of his life and later, under the color of religion, has often become a rationale for massive inhumanity against those who think differently from ourselves.

After Jesus fleshes out "god" as *this* God, we may presume a great deal about his faith, his prayer (Heb. 5:7), his consciousness of his calling, his contemplation in action. Still, you never hear Jesus say unambiguously, "I am God," even though you may assume that the word and work of Jesus are a faithful witness to the God of our fathers and mothers, so much so that, in a very real way, one who denies Jesus and what he is about (e.g., by closing his heart to his neighbor in need, not opening her heart to the God of life), denies the one who sent him (Mt. 25:40 and 45; 10:32-33).

From the nature of the Scriptures it follows that the question, "What *was* Jesus like?" as a request for information on his inner psychology, can put a strain on the Scriptures themselves and cannot be seen as a question motivated solely by faith. Despite all distasteful, time-limited factors, the concern for a dogmatic formulation must go deeper than a quest for information. For christological dogma to be "biblically safe," the Jesus story must ultimately mediate an authentic interpretation of who God is, what God asks of us, and what God needs us for. Then such dogma isn't as far removed from us as it sometimes seems. It is rather the case that our proclamation of what Jesus and God *mean* has often failed. Failed in this sense: the concepts and ideas used have become stale, common, and tired in the hands of dogmatic theologians themselves. These stale concepts cannot embody the touch of the divine mystery that true dogma—living, "solemn teaching" of the church and the Scriptures—should point to. Used woodenly, dogmatic formulae call up a picture, among both outsiders and insiders, of a Christendom whose practice does not convince anyone that God does live and inspire acts of loving kindness, justice, and liberation.

So Jews wonder what Christendom has done with their Old Scriptures and holy places. More and more, they ask, What have you done with "our" Jesus? They read the Book of Daniel, on Jesus' recommendation, and try to understand what they're reading (Mt. 24:15). Those who know Jewish and Israelite history even a little can hardly blame them. Trying to listen to their story with new ears is the least that we can do—humbly take our place on the hard benches of the study house (*bêt ha-midrash*) of Nazareth.

What's New in the New Testament?

Thanks to the prophetic vision of the sixth century BCE and later, forced to confront and find meaning in the destruction of the First Temple and the accompanying Exile (c. 587-538 BCE), a heightened clarity began to be achieved by Israel concerning what its faith tradition was really all about. But during a hard struggle (that spanned five difficult and turbulent centuries) to maintain national existence, circumstances obscured the vision. Important in that loss of clarity was the power struggle for the post of high priest that caused backsliding into older nationalistic mentalities and clinging to the superficial letter of biblical injunctions.

In time, that became a painful business for believers who were not consulted, for example, those in the backward Galilean countryside. Dismayed by the spectacle in Jerusalem, people in the countryside wanted to do something about it. As a result, certain groups took up the search for the essential, the core meaning of the Scriptures. That's why they begin at the beginning, returning to the desert. The Essenes, the authors of the Qumran documents (the Dead Sea Scrolls), and the disciples of the Baptist are all elements of that movement, seeking purity in the face of what they perceived as compromise, politicking, and abuses in Jerusalem.

This is the climate in which the understanding concerning Jesus was discerned and crystallized in the years after his death. In that atmosphere of criticism of the games of powerful urban elites, Jesus was seen as one who had followed the charge to be a witness to the God of the Covenant by realizing the humanity of *this* God. This reconstrual of God entailed a move from taking the prime clues to God's identity from Temple worship and finery to understanding God in terms of "secular" human relationships. It caused fierce protest against Jesus by the leading groups who regarded God as "holy," but who did so in ways that make one suspect they were really trying to safeguard their own positions of influence and privilege.

Jesus' revelation of God radiated from his person; every inch of the Nazarene was the Servant of Isaiah. A small group of ear- and eye-witnesses couldn't keep silent about what they had experienced in accompanying him. He had touched them deeply; they were fully convinced that his God was the One who made Jews Jews and people people. It dawned on them that the whole life of Jesus was a fulfillment of everything written in the Torah, Prophets, and Psalms. And they believed in the Scriptures with new fervor because they had become worth believing in (2 Pet. 1:19). The short-lived "earthly Jesus" first survived in this way, infecting the total life of a small group of people. Even if it were perhaps only unconsciously at first, they stood on their own legs against the structures of the day. They were already thinking of themselves as a faithful "remnant" (Acts 2:40). The internal renewing factor and vision of Israel's faith are there again for all to see.

Then comes the external factor: the destruction of the Second Temple around 70 CE and an even more radical diaspora, which led ultimately to the church of the Gentiles.

What's new about the New Testament rests on two factors. First, in Jesus and the Palestine group gathered around him, the best of the Old Scriptures comes to life again, to such an extent (thanks to their witness) that the Scriptures find a striking and irresistible form in the articulation of and reflection on Jesus' story. With that, secondly, all the dynamic potential of the Jewish religious tradition was available to appropriate and anchor the meaning of a new, intensifying external situation. This difficult process is epitomized in the Council of Jerusalem, recounted in Acts 15.

Jesus in all this is first an historical, empirical fact and person. It is by means of the collage of facts that constitute his life that the sensational stories and interpretations of Jesus recounted by his witnesses are put in motion. There is a first, a second, and even the beginning of a third generation mirrored in the records we have of Jesus. Finally—exhibiting the traces of three generations—we view the completed New Testament, a literary mirror of all those new events. Compared with the thrust of the preceding faith tradition, *the "novum" of the New Testament consists principally in interpreting the message and promise of the Old Scriptures for the peoples of the whole world.* Again, this is not absolutely "new," but a case of the entire life of Jesus intensifying awareness of the universal implications of the Gospel of the God of the Old Scriptures for the well-being and salvation of all peoples. This message is *present* in many strata of the Old Scriptures, particularly in the prophets and Wisdom. It is at the *center* of Jesus' witness.

The Bible for Jew and Gentile

The New Testament doesn't hide its newness under a basket. Rather, it's there on almost every page, because the New Testament is almost constantly involved in controversy, standing up for the nations, the Gentiles.

Doing so caused conflict. In that process, Jesus became a victim. That fact is so central to the New Testament because the countless subsequent conflict situations in which the disciples found themselves took on its color. A lengthy historical controversy involving the church thus becomes concentrated in narratives retelling the story of Jesus. In the Bible, however, this complex of historical and projective elements becomes the theological theme that is an identifying factor for the "new" community of God, one that each believer must be personally taught.

The mistake occurs when people keep reading the Bible as "factual biblical history" centered on certain events. This more or less historical data does belong with the "empirical" material of the Scriptures, with elements of information imparted by Scripture, on the basis of which Scripture imparts valid religious insights. The narrative materials—as exaggerated and pointed as they may be—provide concrete formulations of a theme and are subservient to it. One can, though, so concentrate on the facts as to miss the theme. Then historical or quasi-historical material has overwhelmed the theme, instead of these elements being seen and magnified with eyes of faith.

Take, for instance, "the Jews" in the Fourth Gospel. The point of departure for this theme lies in a real, historical conflict between Jesus and certain Jerusalem circles in the context of various kinds of internal Jewish conflicts. Ultimately, "the Jews" became a standard expression in the completed Gospel of John, a term that achieved a theological significance far in excess of the actual history of the conflict of Jesus and the Johannine Jews. Tragically, that literary expression gave rise to an extraordinarily fatal misunderstanding of Jesus and Jewry, which in no small measure resulted in the Holocaust of 1939-45. In the view being proposed here, however, we only read the Scriptures correctly when we do not over-interpret facts. On the whole, as actual people, the enemies of Jesus were probably no better or worse than the run of persons one encounters on the street today. The point of the recitation of the conflict between Jesus and "the Jews," then, is to help us learn to point our finger at ourselves, not pass on teaching that the Jews are a wicked people.

The New Testament recital of conflict and contrast between Jews and Gentile Christians should leave no stigma or aura of sanctity on either historic group. Such conflict motifs, in fact, are frequently used biblical devices, the purpose of which is really to point the way to the Kingdom, where there is no distinction between "Jew and Greek" (Rom. 10:12). As in the case of the Good Samaritan story (Lk. 10:25-38), the Bible often uses irony as a device to show the danger of prejudices against classes of persons.

In the same way, it can be said that the New Testament is intended to make the Old Testament available for all peoples, not exert a claim for the superiority of Christianity. Jews can still manage quite well with their own Scriptures. In reality, historical events and limitations imposed by history and culture drove them to retreat defensively into their Scriptures and to entrench themselves there. Quite the opposite of a claim commonly made by Christians that, "Whoever has the New Testament has everything," Jews have the right to declare, "Whoever has the Old Scriptures has everything, even the Sermon on the Mount."

Going further, even if it sounds outrageous to many Christians, they can learn much from Jewish belief in the Messiah. Sometimes, I think, Christians must reverse the words of Jesus to experience the true irony of their claims to superiority. The Gospel, you see, is almost always on the side of the weak (a major biblical theme), and you can almost hear Jesus say: "Such great faith have I never found in Christendom." Thematic statements—such as the one we are dealing with on the humility that is indicated by the irony that faith and faithfulness occur in unexpected ways—are themselves far more important in the Scriptures than any endorsement of Christian superiority. To misuse biblical recitations of conflict, as if an historical conflict between Jesus and first-century Jews could be updated to condemn contemporary Jewry, is ridiculous.

So an unavoidable question arises that gives you something to think about: *Who are the more inadequate, Jews who stand outside the Christian tradition, or Christians who misunderstand the permanent, dynamic Jewish contribution to Christianity?* Yet many Christians do not even suspect that this is the case.

Any self-satisfied answer to that question should be distrusted. The break with Judaism, in fact, becomes a break with the Old Scriptures. The Old Scriptures do get read, but because of a poor understanding of the New Testament they are no longer understood. They have been subsumed in Christian themes, twisted out of context, and reduced so drastically that the Christian side of the street looks much wider. That view is an illusion.

What is needed is a long conversion process, preferably beginning at the point at which the estrangement appeared. As a first step I propose the following to Christians: *Cast aside every illusion of Christian superior-*

ity, especially those that claim warrants in the letter of the New Testament, in order to look at the Old Scriptures with new eyes to do them justice and to be able to sense their presence in the New Testament. Wherever people listen to the reason that comes through the same Holy Scriptures—the Old Scriptures discovered anew by Christians, the New Testament made intelligible by Jews—a way opens up to a gradual healing of the most tragic schism in our entire faith tradition.

First and Second Language

Classical biblical language and themes originated primarily in the Israel of the Kings. They functioned at that time within a multifaceted, ancient Near Eastern society. In it both the language and the themes that flowed from the linguistic matrix had a well-defined role in a definite historical context. When this original context and its institutions, which were relativized by the prophets, were seriously altered and eventually disappeared after the two destructions of the Temple, Hebrew and biblical themes began to function more and more as a "sacred" language and themes, memorialized in Scriptures.

There are, for example, national facts such as Israel, Canaan, and its seven peoples (Dt. 7:1; Acts 13:19); David and the first son of David; the Anointed King (the Messiah), Zion, Jerusalem, Liberation from Egypt, the People of God, Holy War, and so forth. Besides such facts as these, there are ordinary, mundane facts: land, water, light, life, bread, word, spirit, heart, countenance, arm, hand, finger, and so forth. The Bible is full of them, and there they can take on a deeper meaning, theological cargo. They become symbols. The realities behind the words pass on from being talked about in *a primary language* of everyday life (that of the house, garden, and kitchen) to become part of *a secondary language*. In that secondary language, ordinary words become suggestive, symbolic evocations of the "surplus of meaning and power" that mark human religious experience. For the good listener, such symbolic terms both point to and excite experiences that await conceptual content and historical definition in an interpretive, discerning moment.

The great misunderstanding concerning the Scriptures can now be concisely expressed. It occurs when secondary language is handled as though it were primary language. This basic communication disorder is, however, a beloved stylistic device in John's gospel (see the conversation with the Samaritan woman, 4:7-15, which hinges on Jesus' play with different levels of meaning for the word "water"). Too often unaware of such ironies, we read the Bible as though empirical biblical history were the point of the narrative.

The transition from Hebrew and Aramaic to Greek sped the process along to Latin and eventually to modern languages. With a certain regret, scholars know that language and images detached from the Hebrew have lost the flexibility of that tongue and that elements such as the fragrance of Canaanite land are gone. On the positive side, though, at the same time, the Scriptures are enriched with Greek meanings and emotive value and power. Still, we have losses such as that illustrated by a title given Jesus in Greek, *pais* (*puer* in Latin, "child" in English, but "servant" in standard English translations) in Acts (3:13 and 26; 4:27 and 30) and in the oldest liturgy (the *Didache*).

Scholars realize that the word is an untranslatable confluence of "child," "boy," "servant," and "son" (see also Lk. 1:54). And so the semantic baggage takes shape, with semiticized Greek as the vehicle. This tongue, although tuned to a concrete religious sensibility, was accessible to the whole known world at that time. Greek, indeed, became the language that mediated the transition made necessary when circumstances led to the Diaspora becoming the mother of a world church.

Three Phases

In the twisting and turning of texts, the dynamic growth process that leads from the local and national functions of texts to "the scriptural function" (as "universally relevant") protects the text from impoverishment. The disappearance of the national framework of pre-Exilic Israel, for example, created the conditions for a broadened and deepened, potentially universal field of meaning, and no biblical word was left out. Words, sentences, and stories tell more than they seem to claim on a surface reading of the text. Getting a hold on, interpreting, fixing this "surplus value," however, requires a definite method and approach. The three-phase division we present below may provide a useful handle. At least it is potentially applicable to the entire scriptural process in Jewish and Christian traditions.

The Jewish phase, as far as the scope of biblical language is concerned, we have been saying, is perfectly homogenous with the New Testament. One even finds that things which some editors of the Hebrew and Greek Bible often sought to repress become more emphatic and openly visible in the New Testament! Ultimately, then, we have distinguished in the scriptural process *an ancient Israelite phase, a prophetic phase, and a Jewish-Christian phase.*

The usefulness of this scheme lies *not* in the neat division of biblical material into three phases, as if that were possible. Although this can be done after a fashion, it requires working at an immensely sophisticated level of literary history that can hardly be demanded of everyone! Those who read the Scriptures and work at a normal level, however, will find it beneficial to assume the influence of all three phases in each bit of biblical writing, whether the elements are in tension with one another or not. An attempt to obtain a feel for how they balance each other out is enriching.

As we have stated, they are there. The national period of linguistic and thematic development, for instance, appears in the present form of every book from beginning to end. It witnesses a non-transferable relationship to Israel's national origins in the land of Canaan, from which Israel derives its deepest sense of meaning.

Prophetic Language

If we work with the present text, the prophetic period assumes a middle or linking position. On the one hand, it is clear that the prophets never completely dropped a residual nationalism even from language that sought to universalize the message of God. On the other hand, the way nationalistic language has been relativized can be read on two levels.

The prophets are not so much interested in the contemporary historic form of the national institutions, whose downfall they proclaim and whose recovery through purification they prophesy. They are much more interested in realizing the *purposes* of those institutions: *making evident God's presence in the midst of humanity*, a presence made evident and even effected by building a society in which Justice and Righteousness reign. That universal vision, according to the prophets' teaching, must be brought about with or without the temple and its sacrifice; with or without a country or language Israelites can call their own; with or without king or capital city.

And this kind of vision and vocation can't be portrayed or accomplished in a straightforward way. "Clarity" cannot be forced. Indeed, this kind of clarity comes about only as a consequence of certainty in the heart.

The texts are so impressive precisely because they have penetrated the blood and marrow of the prophets themselves.

Despite everything, prophets believe that the downfall of all that is old and reliable cannot be the last word about Israel, about Isaac and God, and about the God of the Covenant. The old that is past is known, the new that is to come is elusive; but they use the old in order to put the new into words and images. To look for mere conceptual meaning and clarity is to fail to see that the meaning of the text shifts, and "new meaning" is growing; that the text is dynamic; that it is a vehicle for a surplus of meaning and a springboard for diverse "activity."

With the benefit of hindsight, we can see that this shift in "meaning" results in a different understanding of Scripture than has been common in the Jewish-Christian phase. But this shift to explicit, self-reflective Christian identity does not justify taking meaning, captured so laboriously in later phases, and forcing it onto earlier texts as though it were self-evident to all who call these texts their own.

Incidentally, if caution is indicated when we deal with interpreting what the prophet at such-and-such a time meant to say (as if we had access to his mind), a great deal is possible in interpreting the Bible if the reader does not impose his or her (often highly "spiritual") ideas about God on the Scriptures. Rather, allow the image of God to emerge from the Scriptures. By way of contrast, the accepted norm long seemed to be that the highest level had been reached in texts that dealt with the hereafter and that envisaged an intimate personal relationship with God. Indeed, the scriptural vision in its totality is directed to realizing a state where "God may be all in all" (1 Cor. 15:28). But it is dangerous to envisage that kingdom without envisaging a society in which Justice dwells, for the "real presence" of God ultimately stands or falls on that reality.

This broad vision penetrates all the scriptural material. So it may be rightly asked, What does "the land that I will show you" mean (Gen. 12:1 or Ex. 3:5 and 17) in the light of Isaiah 57:13b or Ezekiel 13:9b or Proverbs 2:21-22? And what does this group mean in the light of Matthew 5:5 or Hebrews 11:9-10, 13-16?

A First and Second Historicity

Therefore it is important that the three phases continue to interact, especially in reading the New Testament. The story that arose, and is gratefully remembered, announcing the First Liberation (from Egypt), in fact, alludes to the Second Liberation of all creation without forgetting its historic roots in an ancient promise. This Second Liberation is what we look forward to in faith. It is this Liberation that is the vocation of faith-filled people to bring to fruition in the whole of creation—in both the human and in other dimensions of life, as we are increasingly reminded by our ecological challenge.

The ancient, national Israelite dimension, which the texts retain through all subsequent reformulations, has fortunately prevented the evaporation of "worldly" dimensions. Most importantly, indeed, that dynamic renders suspect a kind of pervasive over-spiritualization that almost overwhelmed Christian theology. The retention of worldly elements in Scripture, we can see today, has made possible the retrieval of forgotten truths with an earthly and historic scope that many "enlightened moderns" not long ago thought humanity had grown beyond needing. And thus ancient textual elements can be expected to mediate future retrievals. Via such classics and the records of ancient history, we gain access to unsuspected dimensions of our own present-day history and, potentially, to analogous dimensions of all human history. Such texts allude to dimensions of meanings hidden and revealed in mundane, human events. They seek ways to acknowledge what *actually happens* in human existence, what *can happen*, and what *should happen*.

In the same way that a transposition takes place from when texts are read as a first language to being read as a second language, there is a switch from *first* to *second historicity* that is essentially linked to the linguistic shift. The texts have a first historicity in the sense that they hark back to memories that have been passed down, recalling things that once took place. The optics of the biblical book, however, reach much further than the merely empirical, historical past. The world-constructing purpose of "Scripture" is to grip the actual lives of those people whom it addresses by means of the narrative about past events. This transforming objective is in a special way Scripture's real and ever-present historicity, which we are calling the Bible's *second historicity.*

It is an ambiguous fact that the first kind of empirical historicity, so filled with the data of ancient Israel, is almost alone in achieving its purposes. Still, we should be grateful that first historicity texts have maintained their ability to challenge us even today to come to grips with their second historicity dimension—*God is just as much involved in our lives as in the lives of our forebears in faith.*

We have no choice but to live on this earth. The entire biblical proclamation is based on that fact. Our earthly existence is for each of us personal mission and promise of God's providence. Human beings become believers when they discover and meet this God of their own history, when they honor and love God by being faithful to the particular promise and mission that are made possible in their own circumstances. This is not something *individualistic*—although it certainly is deeply *personal.* It's something that we experience together, something we pray for in the second reading of the liturgy of the Easter Vigil, that all the world experience the dignity of being children of Israel's God.

Praesta ut in Abrahae filios
et in Israeliticam dignitatem
totius mundi transeat plenitudo

Grant that all people
throughout the world
might become children of Abraham,
worthy children of Israel.

A Biographical Note

Henri Eduard Jozef (Han) Renckens, member of the Society of Jesus, was born in 1908. In addition to standard Jesuit theological studies, he spent three years in specialized biblical studies under Father (later Cardinal) Augustine Bea. From 1943 through 1967, Father Renckens taught Old Testament at the Jesuit Theological Faculty in Maastrict (The Netherlands), during which time he published three award-winning books: one on Genesis, a second on Isaiah, and a third on the religion of Israel. From 1967 through 1978, Renckens taught at the Catholic Theological University College in Amsterdam. During that period, Father Renckens was deep in dialogue with Amsterdam Jewry and developed themes that fascinated audiences in The Netherlands and Flanders. In this context, in 1984 *A Bible of Your Own* was published in Dutch and has remained in print ever since, with sales demand scarcely slackening.